SIXTEEN
DIFFERENT
FLAVOURS
OF HELL

ISBN 978-1-7353286-0-7 DWFC 226F21
Sixteen Different Flavours of Hell

www.27bslash6.com

By the same author:

The Internet is a Playground
The *New York Times* bestselling first release by David Thorne featuring articles from 27bslash6 plus over 160 pages of new material.

I'll Go Home Then; It's Warm and Has Chairs
The second collection of all new essays and emails.

Look Evelyn, Duck Dynasty Wiper Blades, We Should Get Them
The third collection of new essays and emails.

That's Not How You Wash a Squirrel
The fourth collection of new essays and emails.

Wrap It In a Bit of Cheese Like You're Tricking the Dog
The fifth collection of new essays and emails.

Walk It Off, Princess
The sixth collection of new essays and emails.

Burning Bridges to Light the Way
The seventh collection of all new essays and emails.

Sixteen Different Flavours of Hell
You're holding it.

OFFICE MEMO PRESS

For Jennifer and Mr & Mrs Bus Stop

Alternate Titles for This Book

Please Check Your Calendars

Book 2 of the Knifespawn Trilogy

Five Funerals and a Paddleboarding Lesson

I'd Rather Have Covid Than Josh Gad's Head

Betty Sue's Rickets Medicine

Someone Is That All Probably But I Don't

A Fine Line Between Oblivious and Inanity

Chest Scabies

Walter's Secret Black Family in the Shed

Belligerence Isn't a Sport, Gary

Apple Ear Babies

Barbara's House of Hair and Fridge Magnets

A Lot of People Shit Themselves

Patypuss Bill

Three Crusty Work Gloves and a Didit

Reviews

"I'm sorry I even bothered writing the foreword now."

Ross Amorelli

"I didn't read all of it because it was a bit boring. Definitely not your best. Maybe you should have spent more time writing and less time building a deck. The parts I did read had lots of spelling and grammatical errors. I'm not going to tell you which parts because I hope it goes to print with them."

Ben Townsend

"I suppose I should be thankful you didn't write that I want to tongue-kiss Trump's colon this time."

Mark Shapiro

"I don't offer to take my karaoke machine to every event. That's an outright lie. There's been only ten, maybe fifteen times it's left the house. Besides, people love it."

Holly Thorne

"Little harsh in my opinion. Ease up if you don't mind please."

JM Snell

"It's a bit all over the place. One minute you're talking about telepathic cows and the next you're dissing paddleboards. It's not about standing up, it's about building core strength and balance. Maybe if you tried it you wouldn't have a tummy.

Rebecca Williams

"Is that true about bread? I'm never eating bread again. I mean I'll eat bread, but I'm going to hold it up to a light to check if there's any moths in it first."

Walter Bowers

"It's not exactly Shakespeare. If you're serious about writing, you should consider taking a community college course."

Gary Wright

"I'm fairly sure I've read some of this before. It's like you wrote the book then thought, 'It's a bit thin, I might add some stuff from previous books. Nobody will know.'"

Sally Wedow

"You're such a liar. The book doesn't contain anything about ship building."

Doug Harrop

"I think I may have caught a parasite from the lake. I've had diarrhea for four days so I quit my job."

Rebekah Seifert

"Pfft. Andrew's proposal to Melissa wasn't romantic. All he did was take her camping. How much effort is that? Not that the skanky bitch deserves anything better. You should add something about her teeth."

Jodie Smythe

"I'm only half way through but I've laughed twice."

Sebastian Thorne

"There's no descriptions of me and Jodie. You should write that she's short and fat and that I'm tall and thin. And that Jodie is jealous of me."

Melissa Peters

Contents

Foreforeword

To: David Thorne
From: Ross Amorelli
Date: Friday 23 October 2020 10.12am
Subject: Address

Hey,

I moved from Sydney to Melbourne last week so don't send anything to the old address. I lost my job and broke my foot. I'm thinking about starting my own website like LinkedIn but for people that don't have a job. Any thoughts?

Ross

....

To: Ross Amorelli
From: David Thorne
Date: Friday 23 October 2020 10.18am
Subject: What?

That's a lot to process in one email, Ross. Okay, oh no, and not off the top of my head. How did you break your foot?

David

To: David Thorne
From: Ross Amorelli
Date: Friday 23 October 2020 10.26am
Subject: Re: What?

I don't know. It's just broken.

....

To: Ross Amorelli
From: David Thorne
Date: Friday 23 October 2020 10.28am
Subject: Re: Re: What?

You don't know how you broke your foot? Did you drop something on it?

David

....

To: David Thorne
From: Ross Amorelli
Date: Friday 23 October 2020 10.37am
Subject: Re: Re: Re: What?

I don't think so. What are you doing at the moment?

To: Ross Amorelli
From: David Thorne
Date: Friday 23 October 2020 10.44am
Subject: No.

If you're asking because you want me to build you a website like LinkedIn, I don't have time. I have to finish my latest book in time to meet the print deadline.

David

....

To: David Thorne
From: Ross Amorelli
Date: Friday 23 October 2020 10.51am
Subject: Re: No.

Not like LinkedIn, the opposite of that. What's the new book about?

....

To: Ross Amorelli
From: David Thorne
Date: Friday 23 October 2020 10.56am
Subject: Re: Re: No.

Paddleboards, robot lawnmowers, fridge magnets, Tucker Carlson's hair, telepathic cows. That sort of thing.

David

To: David Thorne
From: Ross Amorelli
Date: Friday 23 October 2020 11.05am
Subject: Re: Re: Re: No.

You should write a book about solar power.

....

To: Ross Amorelli
From: David Thorne
Date: Friday 23 October 2020 11.11am
Subject: Re: Re: Re: Re: No.

Yes, I'll draw on my vast experience working in the solar power industry. I could also include a bonus section on deep sea welding.

David

....

To: David Thorne
From: Ross Amorelli
Date: Friday 23 October 2020 11.18am
Subject: Re: Re: Re: Re: Re: No.

Alternative energy is very popular at the moment. Just saying. Bigger audience than books about cows and fridge magnets. How much more do you have left to write?

To: Ross Amorelli
From: David Thorne
Date: Friday 23 October 2020 11.26am
Subject: Re: Re: Re: Re: Re: Re: No.

Fifty pages or so but I've run out of time so it might be a bit skimpy this year. I still have to write an ending and convince someone to write the foreword on short notice.

David

....

To: David Thorne
From: Ross Amorelli
Date: Friday 23 October 2020 11.32am
Subject: Forward

I'll write the forward for you. I'm not doing anything at the moment.

....

To: Ross Amorelli
From: David Thorne
Date: Friday 23 October 2020 11.37am
Subject: Re: Forward

I appreciate the offer but that's not necessary. It sounds like you have enough on your plate.

David

To: David Thorne
From: Ross Amorelli
Date: Friday 23 October 2020 11.46am
Subject: Re: Re: Forward

You don't think I can write a good forward? I'm a pretty good writer.

....

To: Ross Amorelli
From: David Thorne
Date: Friday 23 October 2020 11.50am
Subject: Re: Re: Re: Forward

You spelled foreword incorrectly in the last two emails, so no, I'm not overly confident.

David

....

To: David Thorne
From: Ross Amorelli
Date: Friday 23 October 2020 11.58am
Subject: Re: Re: Re: Re: Forward

Leave it with me.

I'll throw something together and have it to you in a couple of days.

To: Ross Amorelli
From: David Thorne
Date: Friday 23 October 2020 12.17pm
Subject: Bookdraft.pdf

A couple of days?

I'd like to retract the word 'overly' from my previous email and replace it with 'the slightest bit'. The print deadline is November 16th. If you really want to have a go at writing the foreword, you have until around the 13th of November to get it to me - so three weeks.

I've attached the first hundred pages so you have some idea of the content.

David

....

To: David Thorne
From: Ross Amorelli
Date: Friday 23 October 2020 12.25pm
Subject: Re: Bookdraft.pdf

OK I'm not going to read that much text but I get the general idea.

I don't need 3 weeks to write it. I work best with a tight deadline and I already know what I'm going to write. Thats how I work, I think about stuff for a long time and then do it. Once I start it's usually pretty easy.

To: David Thorne
From: Ross Amorelli
Date: Friday 23 October 2020 6.09pm
Subject: Foreword

OK here's the foreword. I lost my laptop so I did it in wordpad.

Let me know what you think and if it needs to be longer or you need any changes but I think you'll like it.

....

To: Ross Amorelli
From: David Thorne
Date: Friday 23 October 2020 6.26pm
Subject: Re: Foreword

Ross,

It's been less than six hours since you offered to write the foreword. Is this a quick summary of what you intend to write or the actual foreword? It's just random sentences without any structure or flow. Reading it felt like inching forward in traffic. On a bus with grippy brakes.

I'd rather you took your time with it than send me unfinished text. Use the next three weeks to write and rewrite until you're happy with it. There's no rush.

David

To: David Thorne
From: Ross Amorelli
Date: Friday 23 October 2020 6.34pm
Subject: Re: Re: Foreword

I am happy with it. A random flow of thoughts is what I was going for. If I change it or add fluff it will be ruined. Trust me, it's really good.

....

To: Ross Amorelli
From: David Thorne
Date: Friday 23 October 2020 6.47pm
Subject: Re: Re: Re: Foreword

Is it though? The first sentence is, "Hello, my name is Ross." I was expecting that to be followed by, "and this is a story about a floppy-eared bunny named Timmy."

The entire copy reads like you're telling your mum how your day went. It's just "Then I did this" and "Then I did that." You wrote the word 'then' 37 times. I counted. An entire paragraph is devoted to you deciding what to wear, another describes the Washington Monument as "tall and white with a point at the top."

Leave it for a few days and then revisit it. Like I said, there's no rush.

David

To: David Thorne
From: Ross Amorelli
Date: Friday 23 October 2020 7.19pm
Subject: Re: Re: Re: Re: Foreword

I'm not going to revisit it. There's no reason to. It's perfect. Trust me on this. People don't want to read text that's too overly worked. I wrote Hello my name is Ross as an introduction. How else are they meant to know who's writing it and how else would you describe the Washington Monument? It's not round and red.

I wrote it in my voice not yours. If you wanted it in your voice you might as well write it yourself.

Do I get free copies for doing the foreword?

....

To: Ross Amorelli
From: David Thorne
Date: Friday 23 October 2020 7.25pm
Subject: Re: Re: Re: Re: Re: Foreword

It's more of a cry for help than a voice but I'll work with what you've sent. I may need to do a bit of editing though - nobody cares that your legs are muscular.

Yes, you get free copies.

David

To: David Thorne
From: Ross Amorelli
Date: Friday 23 October 2020 7.32pm
Subject: Re: Re: Re: Re: Re: Re: Foreword

The muscular legs bit is important. Why would I be able to walk up so many steps unless my legs were muscular? If you're going to change anything I'd prefer you didn't use it at all to be honest. I only did it to help you out.

....

To: Ross Amorelli
From: David Thorne
Date: Friday 23 October 2020 8.19pm
Subject: Re: Re: Re: Re: Re: Re: Re: Foreword

Understood. I will keep any edits to a minimum and leave in the bit about your muscular legs. I do recognise the effort you put into writing the foreword and my appreciation is proportional.

David

....

To: David Thorne
From: Ross Amorelli
Date: Friday 23 October 2020 8.31pm
Subject: Re: Re: Re: Re: Re: Re: Re: Re: Foreword

You're welcome.

Foreword

By Ross Amorelli

Hello, my name is Ross ███████████████████
██
██
███████████ and █████████████ this ███████
████████████████ is my █████████
███████████████████████████ foreword.
I ████████████ hope
███████████ you ████████ like it █████
████████████ because ██████████████
███████████████████ I spent █████
██
almost ████████████ 2 ██████████████████
██████ hours ███████████████████████████
██
███████ writing it █████████████ then █████
██
██
███████████████ died in an explosion. ██████
███████████████████████ I was ████████
██████████████████ fine though. When David first
asked me to write this foreword, I ███████████
████████████████████████ was ████████████

in a box

growing a beard

and was excited

to let   everyone

know that   he

completes

me   I won't go into details but

he is   like the

best

astronaut or explorer

ever.

you should   see him

jump.   there's nothing

he's incapable of doing

when he's

wearing thick socks and gloves and

he

lives in a house that

is a triangle

David is

also

great at

Venn diagrams and

26

██████ has ████████████ blue ███████

████ pants ████████████ His writing style can best be described as ████████████████████

████████████████████████████████████

██████████████████ salsa - the dance not the dip. ████

████████████████████████████████████

When I visited David and Holly in America they took me to see the Washington Monument in D.C. ████████

████████████████████████████████████

████████████████████ and it ████████

████████ was the best ███████████████

████ day ███████████████ ever ████████

I have a photograph of ███████████████ me ██

████████ holding it up ████████████

████████████████ with my █████

████████████████████████████████████

████████████ arms █████████████████

████████████████████ It's my █████

███████████ favourite ████████████

and █████ I'm ████████████ going to ██████

█████ have it ██████████████████ printed

████████████████████████████████████

████████████████████████████████████

████████████████ onto a █████████

████████████████████████████████████

██████ t-shirt. We also went to New York and I █████

████████████████████████████████████

████████████████████████████████████

████████████████████ drank water infused with fruit.

there was

a banana

so I rented a helmet.

they contain potassium

which doesn't sound safe. You can't see

David and Holly's house from the Empire State Building. I tried

but it was too dark. I should have taken a flashlight. I wish I

was made of

electricity. When I was very young I

was a baby

███████ I have muscular legs ██████████

████████████████████ no ████████ you can't

look ████████████████████

██████████████████████

██████████████████████

██████████████

████████ swish, swish, swish ██████

████████████████████

that's snowboarding for you. ██████████

████████████████████████

████████████████████

████████ I met an Argentinian woman ████

██████████████████████

████████████████████████

██████████████████████

████████████████ Which pretty much sums up

the entire trip.

Chapter 6

To: All Staff
From: Jennifer Haines
Date: Monday 2 March 2020 9.22am
Subject: Calendar update

Good morning everyone,

Just letting you know Mike is hiring a car to drive back from Chicago instead of flying because he's scared of catching Corona. This means he won't be back until Wednesday so I've moved his meetings. Please check your calendars.

As most of you are aware, Mike and I met with Jodie and Melissa and decided to give them another chance. They have agreed to behave in a professional manner as per the employee workplace agreement (4A). It is understood there will be no more warnings. David, I have spoken to you about escalating sensitive situations and I expect you to also conduct yourself in a professional manner.

Could everyone let me know if you're coming for drinks at our house for Dan's birthday. I realize it's still a month away but I need to work out numbers.

Thank you, Jen

There's a bus stop outside my office window. It's on the other side of the road but directly across from the branding agency I work for. It's a sheltered bus stop, with a bench, and every day at 10.15am, an elderly couple arrive, sit, and hold hands while they wait for the bus. They've been doing it since I first started at the agency, so at least ten years. I don't know where they go and I don't know when they return because the bus stop on our side of the street is a few businesses down. I call the elderly couple Mr and Mrs Bus Stop, because I don't know their real names, and I've grown quite fond of them over the years.

"Look, Ben, Mrs Bus Stop has a new wool coat."
"She does?"
"Yes, a red one. I wonder what happened to her yellow one."
"Perhaps she's just mixing it up a bit."
"She's worn the yellow coat every day for four years. You don't just suddenly decide to wear a different coat for no reason. It's nice though. Russian red. Probably PMS 7621."
"Very nice."
"Yes, it goes well with the haircut she got last week."
"It's kind of creepy that you know so much about them."
"No it isn't. It's entirely wholesome. I'm a distant admirer, not a stalker. Besides, I don't *really* know anything about them."
"Looks like the old man has new shoes as well."
"No, he's had those brown brogues for three years, he just shines them well. He probably owns one of those shoe shining kits in a wooden box."

Sometimes, during summer when I have my window open and there's not much traffic, I hear Mrs Bus Stop laugh at something Mr Bus Stop has said. It's a contagious laugh and makes me chuckle. During winter, they snuggle close and Mr Bus Stop puts his arm around Mrs Bus Stop. Earlier this year, on a particularly cold and breezy morning, Mr Bus Stop took off his scarf and wrapped it around Mrs Bus Stop's exposed neck and ears. He then stood and shielded her from the wind.

"She should have worn her own scarf on a day like this."
"Yes, but that's hardly the point, Ben."
"There's no such thing as bad weather, only bad clothing."
"Right you are. Thank you for the wise words, Nanook."
"Why Nanook?"
"I assumed it was an Inuit quote."
"No, it's Norwegian."
"Regardless, Mrs Bus Stop's questionable choice of weather-appropriate attire doesn't detract from the fact that Mr Bus Stop's gesture displays genuine affection and solicitude. I think it's lovely."
"Sure. Now he's probably cold though. It was more of a sacrifice from Mr Bus Stop than a gesture. And selfish of Mrs Bus Stop to accept it. She should have said, 'No, keep your scarf, it was my decision not to wear warmer clothing on a blustery winter day and you shouldn't have to suffer because of it.'"
"Don't you have something else to do, Ben?"
"You called me in here to look at your old people."

For those unaware, there was a global pandemic this year. It began with a scientist having sex with a bat or something. People died, Taylor Swift wrote and released an entire album to make everyone feel bad about themselves, Netflix and PornHub subscriptions doubled, and everyone was asked to wear a mask.

Not everyone wore a mask of course. Some chose to slow the spread of the pandemic and some chose not to partake in what was clearly just another component of the global conspiracy to deprive them of their God-given right to Nascar and Olive Garden 2-for-1 pasta specials.

Having lived in the United States for almost eleven years, one might assume I'd be accustomed to the odd behaviour of Americans. They still manage to surprise me though. Reason and logic are simply hurdles to Americans; some jump over them, some roll under them, and some bypass them altogether by cutting across the field to the finishing line where they declare themselves the winner.

It's a lot like living with three-hundred million toddlers - half of which are the 'stomp your feet until you get all the Lego' type and the other half are the type that eats dirt. That's a generalization of course; there are toddlers who share their crayons, and gifted toddlers who manage not to shit themselves every ten minutes, but the strengths and civic mindedness are, for the most part, drowned out by the stomping, crunching, and shitting.

Balance isn't a thing with Americans, everything is black and white and wrong and right and them and us. There's often a bit of confusion about who the 'them and us' is, but nobody will admit it.

"The stock market has never been higher!"

"Oh, you have stocks?"

"No, but if I did they'd be higher."

"Sure. How are the wife and kids?"

"Doing well. Sharon wrangled a third shift at Waffle House and we received our government stimulus check this week so Betty Sue's rickets medicine is covered."

During an outing to Home Depot recently, I saw an old guy wearing a t-shirt that said, *I don't need a mask, I have Jesus*. There's a cutoff age to wearing graphic t-shirts with logos or messages on them. It's ten. The guy was at the checkout buying a large roll of patterned linoleum - possibly reflooring his trailer with his government stimulus check - and, as is common in this rural region of Virginia, he was open-carrying a handgun on his right hip. The only deduction one can make from this is that protection by Jesus is limited to fending off airborne droplets and, for all other threats, you're on your own.

He looked like the kind of guy who would have exceptional health care coverage though, so I'm sure he'll be fine even if Jesus is distracted for a moment - perhaps to give a child cancer - and misses a droplet.

In Australia - and all other industrialised countries apart from America - we have something called universal health care. Around 2% of your income goes into a 'kitty'. Then, if anyone gets sick or injured, their medical expenses are covered by taking a bit out of the kitty. It doesn't matter if you haven't paid anything into the kitty yet, or are too old or poor to do so, your medical expenses are covered. That way, if little Timmy gets cancer, regardless of his parent's income, he receives treatment, grows up to be a productive member of society, and starts paying his 2% into the kitty.

It's a system that benefits everyone and isn't based on buying health insurance company CEO's their third vacation home in the Hamptons. Nobody goes bankrupt, nobody is denied care, it's less expensive, the quality of care is better, and nobody says, "Timmy's feeling poorly but I'll hold off on taking him to see a doctor because it's so expensive."

America is rated 37th in the world for quality of health care. It's basically a third world country with iPhones and Whole Foods. The American health care system is very similar to insuring a family car - except you're charged Lamborghini rates. It costs several thousand dollars per year and there's generally a deductible. Americans can't wrap their head around a system based on paying less and having everyone covered, because they're happy to pay more if it means someone else doesn't get it for free. Fuck Timmy. His parents shouldn't have had a child if they can't afford to insure it. This isn't a village.

Not everyone in America has to pay for health insurance of course, people who have served in the military and their spouses get free health care for life. For everyone else though, free health care is socialism, and socialism is a dirty word. Socialists are sneaky and lazy and want to turn your children into marijuana smoking homosexuals.

My Republican friend JM smirks and shakes his head if I besmirch the American health care system as anything less than the best in the world. He also thinks the answer to school shootings is to arm all students, that the Trump administration has handled the COVID-19 pandemic well, and that Bigfoot has to be real or there wouldn't be so many television shows about the search for him.

I've explained that having lived in both a country with universal health care, and one without, I'm exactly twice as knowledgeable on the subject than he is, but that's math, which is lost on Republicans. Having only 4% of the world's population, yet 25% of COVID deaths, is easily dismissed with, "That's because there's more people in America."

Regardless, with the 37th best health care in the world - available only to those who can afford it - you'd assume Americans would be taking the pandemic much more seriously than any other country. That they'd be #1 in mask wearing and social distancing, and following CDC guidelines to the letter. Caution is inconvenient though, and unnecessary, because Americans are protected by eagles.

To: All Staff
From: Jennifer Haines
Date: Wednesday 4 March 2020 9.16am
Subject: Mike's meetings

Good morning,

Mike is working from home the rest of the week. He thinks we're all going to infect him with the plague. If anyone else is scared of the Corona virus and wants to work from home you can talk to Mike about it. I'm not going anywhere.

David, can you please set up Mike's laptop so he can use Zoom? His meeting with Kimberly Clark has been moved to next Tuesday and it's now via video. Also, I asked you not to start anything with Jodie and Melissa. Enrolling them in a martial arts workshop isn't being helpful and I don't believe for a second you were trying to be. The company credit card is to be used for work related purchases only.

Melissa and Jodie, you don't have to attend the workshop. The email wasn't from head office. Melissa has expressed interest in the workshop so she may be away on the 12th and 13th.

Walter, please check your emails before sending them to clients. You wrote vagina instead of Virginia twice in an email to Erin last week and she brought it to my attention. You also addressed her as Eric.

Thank you, Jen

This is actually the second pandemic I've lived through. When I was about seven or eight, there was an outbreak of Chickenpox in the small Australian country town my family lived in. This was well before a vaccine was developed and around half the kids at school caught it. Nobody wore a mask or social distanced though. If anything, it was the opposite; we were forced by our parents to have sleepovers and attend 'take your shirts off and wrestle with each other' parties.

"Any spots or itching, David?"
"No, why?"
"No reason. Oh, by the way, you're having a sleepover at Matthew's house tonight. It's all been arranged. No need to take your sleeping bag, you can share his bed."
"Matthew has Chickenpox."
"No he hasn't. They're just goosebumps. Give them a good rub tonight to warm Matthew up."

There was a valid reason for our parents wanting us to catch Chickenpox of course; you can't catch it twice and if you don't catch it when you're young, you're not going to have a good time if you catch it in your thirties. I didn't know this at the time however, and simply assumed my parents hated me and wanted me to suffer. It explained why they wouldn't buy me Moon Boots.

Matthew did have Chickenpox. And Moon Boots. They were the real ones by Tecnica. I eventually got a pair, years later, but they were fake and said Moonbeam Boots on them.

Although Matthew was my best friend at the time, I wasn't a fan of going over to his house. It was a small, two-bedroom home with only a single bathroom, and Matthew's father, Mr Murphy, had killed himself in that bathroom. Apparently he sat in the bathtub, placed the barrel of a loaded rifle in his mouth, and pulled the trigger. Mrs Murphy was out at the time and Matthew was at school - we were in geography class when the assistant principal knocked on the door and asked to speak to our teacher. They spoke quietly in the hallway for a short time, then Matthew was asked to pack up his stuff. I assumed someone had found out about the magazine we'd discovered in his father's shed and whispered to Matthew, "Tell them we found it in the park and there were already pages missing."

My mother and Matthew's mother were, if not friends, then something similar. They were members of the local tennis club and met for coffee occasionally. I learned, years later, that Mrs Murphy, who was a hairdresser, had been having an affair with one of her clients, and Mr Murphy found out about it. At the time, however, I was told he'd shot himself because the Australian cricket team lost an important game to England. It was probably the best way my father could come up with to describe a despondency so bad you wanted to die. He really liked cricket and wasn't big on subtlety. Once, when he and my mother decided to have a trial separation and I asked why, he told me that marriage is like a game of cricket, but without an umpire and with only two players, and one is a bitch.

There were times I did visit Matthew's house, but it was reluctantly and I avoided using the bathroom. If I had to urinate, I'd hold one hand up to my face like a horse blinker to block the bathtub from my field of view. I'm not sure what I thought I'd see, but I'd created a scenario in my mind that when Mr Murphy shot himself, his head exploded and brains and blood and eyes and lips splattered everywhere. And that there'd still be evidence of it.

Years before, my father had repaired a leaking toilet cistern at our house and accidently dropped one of those hockey puck shaped things that turn the water blue onto the floor. Despite the bathroom being scrubbed and bleached many times over the years, the grout between the tiles where the hockey puck thing landed was still stained blue. It was a spot in front of the toilet that you could see between your legs while you were taking a dump. I'd scratch at the grout with a toenail while I was sitting but the colour ran all the way through. At one point, my father scraped out the stained grout and replaced it. The new grout was whiter than the rest and, if anything, stood out worse than the stained grout had. Then, over the space of a few months, the new grout took on a blue tinge.

I imagined that's how it would be with brains and blood and eyes and lips. It wouldn't matter how hard you scrubbed the grout, or how many coats of paint you layered the walls and ceiling with, one day you'd be sitting in the bath and notice everything has a tinge of pink.

Before school one morning, my mother told me to go to Matthew's house that afternoon so Mrs Murphy could give me a haircut. I think it was for a bit of extra cash on the side because I usually went to Barbara's House of Hair & Fridge Magnets for my six-dollar haircuts.

Barbara's House of Hair & Fridge Magnets was originally just called Barbara's House of Hair but at some point Barbara decided to branch out and start selling art from the salon. At first it was just paintings of her Boston Terrier and Jesus, with a few landscapes of the local area and portraits of clients, but then Barbara tried her hand at Aboriginal art. Barbara wasn't Aboriginal - she was a short, thin, white lady in her seventies with blue rinsed hair - but she managed to create fairly decent dot-based representations of kangaroos and emus on pieces of bark. As our town was off a main tourism road, the paintings practically sold the moment the paint had dried. Discovering she was making a lot more money from the bark paintings than haircuts, Barbara changed the name of her shop to Barbara's House of Hair & Aboriginal Art until a local Aboriginal artist, an actual Aboriginal, took Barbara to court for cultural appropriation and misrepresentation. Barbara agreed to stop forging indigenous artwork and dropped the word Aboriginal from the name of her shop. For a while it was called Barbara's House of Hair & Art, but I guess she sold more hot-glued felt koala fridge magnets than paintings of her Boston Terrier and Jesus, and decided to corner the hair and fridge magnet market.

Often when I was having my hair cut at Barbara's House of Hair & Fridge Magnets, the bell on the door would jingle and tourists would enter looking puzzled and Barbara would say, "Haircut or fridge magnets? If you're looking for Aboriginal art, I have some out back. I can't display it in the front of the shop because the local blackie gets his knickers in a knot."

The 'local blackie', perhaps inspired by Barbara's initial success in the Aboriginal art market, opened his own gallery a few shops down from Barbara's House of Hair & Fridge Magnets. His dot-based kangaroo and emu paintings weren't as good as Barbara's though, and the gallery closed after only six months. It became a café, then a shoe store, and finally a newsagency. There was another newsagency in town so it caused a bit of a turf war; bricks were thrown through windows, rumours were started that the new newsagency owner was a homosexual, and there was even a brawl between the two newsagents at an under-14s football game. Snacks and drinks were thrown and one of the newsagents ripped a windscreen wiper off the other's car and chased him with it. The altercation made front page of the local newspaper and, in the photo they used, Matthew and I could be seen in the background sitting on our bikes. We were pretty much famous for a couple of days and I cut out the photo and had it taped to my bedroom wall until my sister, Leith, obviously jealous, added a voice bubble coming from my head stating, "I'm a girl," because my hair was getting a bit long.

"Hello, Mrs Murphy. Mum told me to come over after school to get a haircut."

"Yes, David, I have it all set up for you. I saw your photo in the newspaper by the way. Very nice."

"Thanks."

"Well, head into the bathroom and we'll get started."

"The bathroom?"

"Yes, it can get a bit messy."

"You could cut my hair outside. It's a nice day."

"Yes, it is, but there's no plug outside for the clippers."

"You could run an extension cord out there."

"Don't be silly, come along. I've put a kitchen chair in the bathtub for you to sit on."

Mr Murphy had worked for the Australian Parks & Wildlife Service, it's why he owned a rifle I suppose. He also drove a white government-issued Land Cruiser with four-wheel drive. As such, there were plenty of secluded spots in the Australian outback he could have driven to and shot himself. Maybe it was a spur of the moment decision, or maybe he wanted to stain the grout, to make a statement that couldn't be scrubbed away. It had been though. There were no remnants of brains and blood and eyes and lips on the bathroom tiles, no pink tinge. The tiles and grout were sparkling clean, as if new - as if it had never happened. I'd feared something that wasn't there, blinkered myself and drawn out that fear far longer than was necessary. Once when I'd needed to poo, I ran home to do it and shit myself on the way.

It works both ways of course, people often blinker themselves from situations that should be faced - situations that are a danger to themselves and others.

"Do you actually know anyone that's been eaten by a shark, David?"
"Well, no, JM, but..."
"Exactly. And that's why I swim in the ocean with hotdogs taped to my body. Because sharks don't exist."

Part of the reason is optimism bias, the belief that bad things only happen to other people, but consensus bias, the belief that one's choices and judgments are common and therefore appropriate, plays a major role. It's especially prevalent in group settings where one thinks the collective opinion of the group matches that of the larger population, and that anyone who doesn't agree with their choices and judgments is an idiot.

"Stop spreading fear. Babies are very resilient. If you cut off their ears and replace them quickly with apples, there's very little blood loss. People have a right to apple ear babies."
"It just doesn't make any sense."
"Tell that to all the people in the apple ear babies Facebook group I'm a member of."
"Don't the apples rot?"
"Eventually, sure, but you just swap them out when that happens. Stick new apples on. Or little pumpkins for fall and avocados for Cinco de Mayo."

To: All Staff
From: Jennifer Haines
Date: Thursday 5 March 2020 11.01am
Subject: PARTY!
To: All Staff

From: Jennifer Haines
Date: Thursday 5 March 2020 11.16am
Subject: Re: PARTY!

Walter, thank you for doing the invite but Mike pointed out that gifts is spelled incorrectly. Could you fix please?

Thank you, Jen

If someone had asked me a year ago what I thought the consequences of a worldwide pandemic might be, I may have guessed some kind of *Mad Max* scenario with factions fighting over gasoline, cigarettes, and Keurig cups. Or maybe, and I realize it's a stretch, everyone acting like decent human beings and following logical scientific advice to get through the pandemic as quickly as possible with the least number of deaths. I never would have guessed 'the politicization of mask wearing'. It seems absurd that performing the simplest of tasks to protect yourself and others from a potentially fatal disease could be argued against, and, honestly, you'd assume the ones refusing to wear masks would be the first to embrace them as their teeth would be hidden.

It's possible at this point you may be declaring, "'Merica, bitch. There's no scientific evidence that masks work and there's nothing wrong with my tooth!" but I can't hear you, this is a book.

Early in the pandemic, before it was even called a pandemic, I asked my coworker Ben what he'd do if the virus got really bad and he told me he'd go to a deserted island to wait it out. Which sounds nice but I'm not sure how he'd get there or how he'd survive. He has no boating experience, I've seen him freak out over a moth in his office, and he doesn't eat meat or fish. Once, during a client lunch, Ben discovered a bit of bacon in his salad and started gagging so badly he couldn't breathe and had to lie on the floor. What's he going to eat on his island? Bark?

"What are you going to eat on your island, Ben? Bark?"

"No, I'll eat coconuts. They're high in protein and fibre."

"I'm sure they are. Plus you can make monkeys out of the shells when you get bored. For company."

"I won't be bored, I'll be too busy doing island things."

"Like what?"

"Swimming and relaxing."

"Well that sounds nice. Ignoring the fact you don't own a boat and have no navigation experience, I'm surprised you haven't left already."

"If the virus gets bad, I'll just steal a boat."

"You'll steal someone's boat?"

"Yes, from a jetty."

"And just point it out to sea, hit go, and hope you come across an island with coconuts?"

"I have Google Maps."

I asked the same question of a few other coworkers. Walter stated that if civilization collapsed he'd go camping and live off squirrels, Jennifer said it was an unrealistic scenario because it's just like a bad case of the flu, and Gary said, "If it means never having to listen to idiotic conversations about coconut islands again, I hope I catch Covid and die."

Rebecca had the only viable plan; she'd head to her father's cabin to wait it out. When Rebecca's mother passed away from cancer five years ago, her father sold the family home, purchased five acres of lakeside property, and had a wood cabin built. Apparently it has solar panels and a water purification system so, if you had enough supplies or liked to fish, you could theoretically hunker down there indefinitely. Rebecca's father spent his days fishing, cutting firewood, and writing a novel about a sentient crab, until he had a heart attack while trying to pull-start the motor on his dinghy.

It was a couple of weeks before Rebecca drove up to check why he wasn't answering his phone or emails, so I assume it was a closed casket. Rebecca planned to keep and use the property for a year or two, then sell it. She invited everyone from work to spend the 4th of July there last year and, while I didn't go, I still have the address she emailed me. As such, Rebecca's plan to head to her father's cabin if the shit hits the fan is also my plan. I'll get there first and change the locks.

"Let me in, I have nowhere else to go."
"Perhaps you should have thought about that before you told Mike I forged his signature to order an office parrot."

When I was in grade eight or nine, our class watched a movie called *The Day After*, about a nuclear attack and the aftermath that follows. There's a scene where a family is in a bunker or basement rationing food, and, after watching the movie, our teacher had us write an assignment about who we'd let in to our bunker if space and food was limited, and why. Most of the class wrote that they would include their parents, siblings, friends and pets - maybe their grandparents and relatives. I chose Jeannie from *I Dream of Jeannie* and I still stand by my choice.

These days, if I had to choose who to let into a bunker, excluding Anne Hathaway and television genies, I'd probably only include my partner Holly and my offspring Seb. Even those two are iffy. Seb eats and shits his own weight every few hours, and Holly would want to bring the dogs, Trivial Pursuit, and her karaoke machine into the bunker. I'd rather stay outside and take my chances to be honest.

"Who's up for karaoke?"
"Actually, I was just about to head out. Might scavenge for food amongst the ruins while fending off giant mutant radioactive cockroaches for a bit."
"How long will you be?"
"That depends on whether I'm captured by post-apocalyptic warlords or not."
"Okay. Bring back some toilet paper. We're almost out."

Another consequence of a pandemic that I never would have guessed, is a worldwide shortage of toilet paper. For a while rolls were disappearing off supermarket shelves as fast as the supermarkets could stock them. I've seen dozens of movies and television shows about global pandemics and not once in any of them did someone state, "Oh no, we're out of toilet paper, I'll have to take a shower after I poo."

"Rick, walkers have breached the perimeter walls... Rick?"
"He's taking a shower."
"Now?"
"Big lunch."

To: All Staff
From: Jennifer Haines
Date: Monday 9 March 2020 9.47am
Subject: Toilet paper

Good morning,

Just letting everyone know we're running low on toilet paper. I brought in a couple of rolls from home and Melissa is trying to find some online, but until then everyone needs to be frugal. Please don't use paper towels as it blocks the toilet. If you do block the toilet, please unblock it for the next person. Nobody should have to use the plunger on someone else's poo. I'm not pointing fingers at anyone, Gary, but I will if it happens again.

Melissa and Gary will be away this week on the 12th and 13th. Please check your calendars. Gary, Mike approved your purchase request for athletic pants and sneakers.

David, Mike is fine with you working remotely. He thought you had been for the last 3 years. Please be here for the Friday production meetings though.

Walter, please read your emails twice before clicking the send button. Japanezy isn't a word and "someone is that all probably but I dont" isn't a sentence. Please use capitals and punctuation and sign off with your name and email signature instead of just writing "bye."

Thank you, Jen

I know a guy named Mark Shapiro who purchased two thousand rolls of toilet paper a week before they disappeared from shelves - which is kind of selfish and reeks of insider knowledge; his ex-girlfriend, Emily, used to work for the Center for Disease Control in Atlanta. Or she was quarantined there, I can't recall the exact details. A strain of bacteria found in damp dumpsters is named after her.

Mark has a new girlfriend now, named Brie, like the cheese, and she has approximately twelve offspring of various shape, size, and hair colour. They met on Tinder after Mark upgraded to Tinder Plus for $19.99 per month, which gives him unlimited swipes. I've never used Tinder, so I'm no expert on how it works, but I assume swiping right on every female aged between 21 and 99 in a fifty-mile radius upped Mark's chance of finding that 1 in 6,946.

I'm not a huge fan of Brie - Mark's new girlfriend, not the cheese - as she acts like Mark's house is hers and makes me take off my shoes before entering. Prior to the two dating, Mark kept a blue Lowe's bucket in his living room for when he couldn't be bothered walking all the way to the kitchen sink to urinate. It also served as a bottle cap depository and ashtray. Now you're not allowed to smoke in Mark's house because one of Brie's offspring has asthma. How is that anyone else's problem? Buy the kid a snorkel and tape a sponge to the end. I have to put my shoes back on every time I want to have a cigarette and then take them off again. It's just inconsiderate.

I'm not a fan of the cheese Brie either. It's pale with a grayish tinge under a rind of white mould. I'll take a Kraft single over mouldy or sloppy soft cheeses any day. I don't care if that makes me a cheese philistine. Enjoy your mouldy grey cheeses and sloppy soft ones that look like baby vomit, I'll have a bit of Colby Jack if I'm feeling adventurous.

I read somewhere that blue vein cheese only became a thing during the Dark Ages when the inhabitants of a besieged castle ran out of food, were forced to eat mouldy cheese, and declared, "Not bad. I definitely prefer this over rat."

"Barry, try this cheese, it's delicious."
"No thanks, it's mouldy. I realise we're besieged and have run out of food but that doesn't mean we have to resort to eating rancid scraps. Is there anything else?"
"Just this pitcher of milk. It's curdled and gone blobby and smells a bit, but it tastes pretty good. Kind of like a sloppy soft cheese. Try it."
"No, I'm good."
"Suit yourself. By the way, how are the wife and kids?"
"They're fine. They have the plague but the King says it's just like a bad case of the flu and will go away in the warmer months like a miracle."

Incidentally, Brie, Mark's girlfriend, is also pale with a grayish tinge but that's probably from having twelve offspring and spending a lot of time in a house where all the windows are blocked by monolithic toilet paper stacks.

"Shoes off."

"Really, Mark? My soles are clean. Look."

"Doesn't matter, Brie might drop past without warning."

"Fine."

"Come in, have a seat."

"Where?"

"There's a chair in the corner, behind the pyramid of Charmin Ultra Strong. Just make your way through the valley of Cottonelle Ultra ComfortCare and turn left at Quilted Northern Peak."

"Was Costco having a sale on toilet paper?"

"No, just stocking up in case."

"In case of what? A six-month bout of explosive diarrhea?"

"No, the Corona thing."

"Ah."

"Yes, apparently it's just like a bad case of the flu and will go away in the warmer months, like a miracle, but you can never be too prepared."

"And your idea of being prepared is to buy a thousand rolls of toilet paper?"

"Two thousand. It took thirty-four trips in my Fiat."

"But why toilet paper?"

"To beat the panic buyers."

"Nobody is going to panic buy toilet paper. It's stupid."

"Well don't come running to me with a dirty bum when you run out of toilet paper and the supermarket shelves are empty."

"I won't be running anywhere with a dirty bum. If for some inexplicable reason there *is* a shortage of toilet paper, I'll just take a shower after I poo."

"You're going to take six or seven showers every day? How big is your water heater?"

"I've no idea. You poo six or seven times a day?"

"On average. Sometimes more, sometimes less if I'm busy. How many poos do you do a day?"

"One."

"Wow. That's not normal. You should see a doctor."

I'm fairly sure six or seven bowel movements a day isn't normal but the following week, at Deer Camp, Mark asked my friend JM how many times a day he poos and, as majority rules, it was decided that anything less than five poos a day is cause for concern, and that I most likely have some kind of 'reverse' irritable bowel syndrome and could actually pop. It was also established that weighing the same as a tractor with a backhoe attachment doesn't attribute to the daily poo disparity in any way, and that making such a comparison was rude and uncalled for and JM had actually recently lost thirty pounds.

In my defence, as an Australian who was taught the metric system in school, the only way I can calculate weight in the United States using the imperial system is to compare it to common objects. I know eighty pounds is a big bag of concrete so I just base everything off that: Forty pounds is half a big bag of concrete, ten pounds is a cat, twenty pounds is two cats, and a tractor with a backhoe attachment is more than my vehicle can tow.

I have no idea who came up with the imperial system but I would have liked to have been there when the idea was pitched.

"Look, it's simple. Three barleycorns is an inch, twelve inches is a foot, three feet is a yard, twenty-two yards is a chain, ten chains is a furlong, eight furlongs is a mile, and three miles is a league."
"It's a bit all over the place."
"No it isn't."
"How am I meant to remember all those different numbers?"
"You're not, it's impossible. Just remember the first few."
"What if someone needs to measure something smaller than a barleycorn?"
"That's the beauty of the inch, it's divided into sixteenths."
"Right. And what are those increments called?"
"One sixteenth of an inch."
"Or one fifth and a third of a barleycorn?"
"Why are you trying to make this more difficult than it is?"
"I'm not, I'm just trying to wrap my head around it. Explain the weight thing again."
"Okay, twenty-seven grains is a scruple, three scruples is a dram, fifteen drams is an ounce, sixteen ounces is a pound, fourteen pounds are a stone, and one-hundred and forty-three stone is a ton."
"You're just making it all up as you go along, aren't you?"
"No."
"I'm fairly sure you said boople the first time, not scruple."
"No, I didn't."

To: All Staff
From: Jennifer Haines
Date: Monday 16 March 2020 3.06pm
Subject: Update

Good afternoon,

As most of you are aware, Mike, Ben, David and Walter are now working remotely from home. This is not a permanent arrangement and it doesn't mean everyone can work remotely. If you're scared of catching Covid, by all means wear a mask but be respectful of other people's choices.

Ben, your timesheets show you spent 52 hours on the Lasko packaging copy. The billable hours quoted for this were 4. David, just because you're working from home doesn't mean you don't have to do your timesheets. Writing 'stuff' and 'other stuff' doesn't help anyone.

Melissa, as laid out in the employee workplace agreement, (section 4C), telling Jodie that you could crush her windpipe with one punch is threatening behavior and against company policy. Everyone has a right to feel safe in the work environment.

Walter, please have someone check your emails before you send them to clients. You cannot write, "K I will fuck with it a bit and C if that works" to the marketing director of Marriott. You also spelled your own name wrong.

Thank you, Jen

It was the first time I'd been to Deer Camp in several months. Seb and I used to look forward to riding ATVs around JM's large wooded property; we'd explore new trails and get stuck in muddy bogs and have to pull each other out with a chain. Afterwards, we'd drink beer around a roaring campfire with JM and others and laugh at exaggerated stories. Eventually, there were no new trails to be explored, we knew the depth of all the muddy bogs, and the exaggerated stories had all been heard. There was still a camaraderie and the enjoyment of being out in nature, but the exaggerated stories around the campfire became arguments over politics until we agreed not to discuss politics. Now we just sit around the campfire in silence, avoiding politics, until someone thinks of something to say that won't end with JM storming off to his tent yelling, "The South will rise again!"

"Thirty pounds? Damn, JM. That's like three cats or half a bag of concrete. One of the sixty-pound bags of concrete obviously, not the big bags which weigh eighty pounds. Still, well done, I wouldn't mind losing a cat or two from my stomach."

"You just have to exercise and stick to a diet."

"If only there was a pill you could take. One that you swallow before bedtime and wake up buffed."

"You don't need a pill, you just need to exercise and stick to a diet."

"Or mind transfer."

"Sorry?"

"Some kind of device where someone swaps minds with you, someone physically inclined, and they exercise and diet while your mind is cached on a hard drive for a few weeks. It's 2020, we should have things like that by now. Why are people wasting time inventing Pad Pillows when we don't have mind transfer yet?"

"What's a Pad Pillow?"

"It's a special pillow to put your iPad on while you're lying in bed. Holly bought one and it's stupid."

"I'd be happy to email you my exercise and diet plan if you'd like."

"Why are you trying to fat shame me?"

"I'm not."

"Okay, let's talk about something else. Something other than my stomach."

"I bought a new set of tent pegs last week."

"You did? Are they nice?"

"They're okay."

"That's good. What else should we talk about? Did the tent pegs come with ropes?"

"No, just the pegs... how the fuck would you know how much a tractor with a backhoe attachment weighs?"

"I thought about getting one earlier this year. There was one listed on Craigslist that looked nice, it was blue, but apparently you can't just ride a tractor with a backhoe attachment home, you have to tow it on a trailer."

"What do you need a tractor with a backhoe for?"

"To dig holes."

"Buy a shovel. Have you ever used a backhoe before?"

"No, but I've driven a tractor."

"You'd be better off getting a Bobcat."

"Yes, that would be cool. Holly would never agree to it though. I wanted an alligator last year but she said it would eat the dogs."

I was eight when I drove a tractor. Technically I just steered it while sitting on a farmer's lap but it still counts. It was on one of those 'pick your own strawberries' farms. I wrote about the experience for a 'what I did on school break' assignment a few weeks later, but left out the part about the farmer being on the tractor with me and added something about rescuing a lost lamb.

My English teacher, Mrs Bowman, could have just left it, but decided to call me out about why the farmer would let me drive off on a tractor by myself, and how I knew how to throw a lasso to drag the lamb out of quicksand. I told her the farmer was busy planting corn and I learned lasso twirling from my uncle, who was a cowboy, but she called bullshit and brought in a rope the next day for me to demonstrate to the class.

Surprisingly, I was naturally gifted at rope handling and managed to lasso a chair from across the room. My classmates cheered and the teacher apologised for doubting my story and gave me an A for my assignment. Later that day, I saved a school bus full of children from going over a cliff by lassoing the bumper just in time.

No, not really, when presented with the rope, I mumbled something about it not being the right kind for lassoing, and Mrs Bowman instructed me to sit down and told a story to the class about a boy who lies and doesn't find money behind dusty jam jars so can't buy a bike.

I can't recall the exact details of the story but basically a boy, apparently named David, is saving up to buy a bike. He asks a farmer if he has any chores he needs doing and the farmer tells David that if he changes the straw in the chicken coop and cleans the dust off a high shelf of jam jars, he will pay David two dollars. David agrees to what is essentially child labor and heads off to the chicken coop. There was a lot of straw so David, figuring the farmer wouldn't be able to tell the difference, just throws some new straw on top of the old straw to save himself some work. He then heads to the special shelf where the farmer keeps his jam jars, and dusts only the ones in front that are visible. Thinking he's oh so clever, David heads back to the farmer, states that he has finished the chores, and asks to be paid. The farmer puts on an act about being puzzled, because he left the money on the job sites, and makes David follow him back to the chicken coop where he lifts up the straw, new and old, and shows David a dollar on the dirt. The farmer then checks the jam jars and shows David a dollar inside a dusty jar at the back.

At this point, anyone else would have said, "Weird that you were able to set all that up before I even asked you about doing chores, but okay, you got me, keep your two dollars you trap-setting old cunt," but apparently David just hung his head in shame and walked home. Also, the next day, David asked several different farmers if they had any chores for him to do, but word had gotten around about his half-arsedness and David never got his bike. Or he learned his lesson and eventually got his bike. I can't remember how the story ended, or what the point of it was, probably not to trust farmers.

It's true, you can't trust farmers. Once, when our class went on an excursion to a dairy farm, a farmer told me cows communicate to each other telepathically and I believed it for several years. I mean, why would a farmer make that up? Sorry your job is so boring you have to lie to eight-year-olds but perhaps you should consider the repercussions of when they're fourteen and arguing with a biology teacher because they were given false information by a professional in the milk industry.

Being well into her eighties, Mrs Bowman often dozed off at her desk during class; awakening only when her neck snapped back or the school siren sounded. Sometimes we were able to pack our stuff quietly and give ourselves an 'early minute' without stirring her. Once, after rolling the television on wheels into class and putting on *Murder on the Orient Express* for us to watch, Mrs Bowman dozed off in the first five minutes so we swapped the video cassette and watched *Moonraker* instead. One day she didn't wake up. And shit herself.

The older I get, the more I understand the whole dozing off thing. I haven't seen the end of a movie in years. Sometimes I'll jolt myself back awake when I hear myself snore, other times I'll do a quick analysis of the pros and cons of napping at that moment. Driving? Probably best to be awake. Watching a Netflix show that Holly has selected? I don't need to know if the edgy teen lesbian goes to the prom to confront her best friend about the kiss or not. I'm sure it will work out fine. Holly blames my naps on never getting a good night's sleep - due, apparently, to needing a new mattress and not because Holly sleeps sideways and thrashes about like she's doing calisthenics. Forget the whole 'stealing the blanket' thing, try sharing a bed with someone who rolls up in it like a huge cocoon and uses their legs to push themselves around in circles while mumbling, "Come on, we can win this," and "That's not how you swim, you have to use your legs like this."

Holly dragged me mattress shopping recently but there's no way I can properly test how comfortable a mattress is when the salesman is standing a foot away staring down at me. It's just weird. I don't care if it's a coil-foam hybrid, go sit behind your sad little desk and contemplate the mistakes you made in life that brought you to this point. I'll come and get you when I want to know if you have a mattress as comfortable as the ten-thousand dollar Hästens Excelsior, but for around the four-hundred dollar mark. Don't get me started on Sleep Number, I'm not paying that much for a blowup mattress. Coleman sells them for forty bucks.

It may be a terrible thing to admit, as I'm known for my empathy and kindheartedness, but I was glad when Mrs Bowman died. I didn't consider how her death might affect her family and loved ones, I only saw it from a personal perspective and how it affected me. It meant not having to read *The Diary of Anne Frank*. I'm sure it's a fine book and hats off to Anne for inventing Braille, but I was into science fiction at that age and couldn't care less about a deaf and blind girl hiding in a wardrobe.

I've never been a fan of 'the Classics'. I once had to read Alcott's *Little Women* for a school assignment and I figure that's enough of the Classics to keep me going for a while. It mainly consisted of girls talking about their feelings and complaining about things. There was also a guy who rode a horse.

Our principal held an assembly the next day and asked us to close our eyes and bow our heads for a minute of silence to remember Mrs Bowman's 'bright smile and love of teaching'. I'm fairly sure she hated teaching and her teeth were the colour of banana skins. The worst thing that could happen to you in class was for Mrs Bowman to lean over your desk to explain something as her breath smelled like cat food. You learned to hold your breath but if she hovered too long, you risked blacking out and eventually had to inhale. Once she used my pen and put the end in her mouth so I had to throw it away. I was pretty cross about it because it was a Kilometrico.

I kept my eyes open during the minute of silence, as both a way of defying authority and a sign of disrespect, and glanced across at my friend Matthew. He too had his eyes defiantly open because Mrs Bowman once told a story about a boy, named Matthew, who never washed his hair and only had puppets for friends.

There was talk of changing the name of the school library from The Hansard Library to The Edith Bowman Library, but the family who donated money for the library to be built, and for which it was named, caused a bit of a stink so the school cafeteria was named after Mrs Bowman instead. They put up a new sign, and a framed photo of Mrs Bowman eating a sandwich during Sports Day, and Mr Bowman attended the ribbon cutting. He looked slightly bewildered by the whole thing but posed for a photo behind the counter serving a student a sausage roll.

Mrs Bowman's replacement, Mr Mudge, had us write a single page essay about what Mrs Bowman meant to us as an assignment. I wrote a story about a witch being burned alive by villagers because her breath killed their crops.

Also, when Mr Mudge replaced Mrs Bowman, his daughter Georgina enrolled at the school. I think their family must have moved from a rural area because Georgina complained about missing her horse. I was rather smitten with Georgina - she wore glitter lip gloss - so, to impress her, I told her that I owned a horse and knew how to throw a lasso.

Matthew also had a thing for glitter lip gloss and told Georgina I'd made the whole thing up, so, to prove I wasn't lying, I invited Georgina to go horse riding that weekend. It was a Monday, which gave me five days to come up with a viable excuse to cancel, but Georgina told her father, who informed me he was going to call my parents to confirm a time to come over, and I panicked and said that my horse, Knight Rider, caught foot and mouth disease from a cow and had to be shot.

A few weeks later, to reengage Georgina's attention, I told her I was having a birthday party and that she could come if she wanted. It was nowhere near my birthday and I have no idea why I said it was. Word quickly got around and, cornered by the lie, I confirmed to around twenty kids that yes, I was having a birthday party and yes, they could come. I was enjoying the attention at this stage. To add realism, I provided each a sheet from a pad of party invites with my address and a date set several weeks away, again figuring this would give me plenty of time to think of a reason to cancel. I forgot all about it until the first guests arrived. My father was watching cricket on television while my mother was out doing the weekly shopping.

I pretended there'd been a mix-up and I'd accidently written the incorrect day and month on twenty invites but I don't think anyone bought it. Also, one of the kids asked my father if he was really a motorcycle stunt man and if they could see his rocket-bike in the shed.

To: All Staff
From: Jennifer Haines
Date: Wednesday 18 March 2020 1.49pm
Subject: Mike's meetings

Good afternoon all,

Just a quick reminder that those who are working from home are still expected to be available during work hours.

David, I tried ringing you today at 11.30am and was sent to voicemail. I left a message for you to call me back but didn't hear from you so I rang again at 1.30pm and Holly answered your phone. She told me you were having a nap and she didn't want to wake you because you get angry when she does. You wouldn't be sleeping at the office so please sleep on your own time.

The same goes for everyone. Walter, we are friends on Facebook so you can't tell me you are working on the Scotts grass seed packaging and then post pictures 15 minutes later of you and your friend Jackson riding mountain bikes down a hill. The artwork is due Friday.

Still waiting on a few of you to get back to me about Dan's birthday party. The DJ cancelled due to the pandemic but Holly has kindly offered to bring her karaoke machine so that should be fun.

Thank you, Jen

Before the pandemic, my friend Ross visited from Australia. We saw the statue of Abraham Lincoln from *Planet of the Apes*, did the Empire State Building thing, shot guns, and rode a pig. We also took a range of illegal substances because Ross has an ongoing challenge with himself to see how much, and how many, foreign substances his body can handle without dying. If he had a catchphrase, it would probably be, "Fuck my metabolism, that much would have killed anyone else."

During one of our outings, we came across a small bar. It was in the middle of nowhere and most of the clientele were rednecks in their sixties or older, nursing pints and smoking cigarettes at tables pocked with scorch marks. The interior was dimly lit by neon Coors Lite and Pabst Blue Ribbon signs and, on a small stage towards the back, an old lady wearing a hair net was belting out Dolly Parton's *Jolene* on a karaoke system.

"Oooh. Karaoke! We're definitely doing that."
"Really, Ross?"
"Yes, after I've finished my beer. You're not going to sing?"
"No, I don't know any farm emo songs and I'll probably be lynched if I sing anything else."
"Well, Holly will do karaoke with me, won't you Holly."
"Fuck no."
"Weak. Do you think anyone will care if I do a line of coke here or should I go to the bathroom?"
"Probably best to keep it low key."

Hair net lady followed up *Jolene* with another three or four Dolly Parton songs, and Ross got a bit annoyed and said that there should be a limit on how many songs you can sing before it's someone else's turn. Nobody else seemed to mind though, they clapped and yelled, "Sing another one, Hair Net Lady!" They didn't actually call her Hair Net Lady but I can't remember what her name was. The moment Hair Net Lady exhausted the Dolly Parton playlist and sat down, Ross leapt to the stage. He flicked through the list of songs available, frowned, then shrugged and made a selection. The opening chords to *Don't You Want Me* by The Human League flooded the bar. A couple of patrons looked up from their beers and frowned, but a woman wearing a bedazzled denim jacket screeched, "Ooh, I love this song!"

Pleased by the positive reaction to his song choice, Ross opened with, 'Okay, this one goes out to the lady with the denim jacket," and amended the lyrics to, "You were wearing a denim jacket in a smoky dark bar, when I met you..."

His tonal range wasn't great but Ross received a decent amount of applause. Mostly from Holly and I, but denim jacket lady chipped in and gave him one of those whistles some people can do with their fingers. Nobody yelled, "Sing another one, Beard Boy!" but he did anyway. Mid way through the murder of Soft Cell's *Tainted Love*, Holly turned to me and said, "That actually looks like fun."
"You should have a go then," I told her.
"Maybe," Holly nodded.

Holly had never sung karaoke before. She hummed and hawed about doing it, you could tell she wanted to, but after Ross relinquished the stage, it remained empty.

"Nobody wants to follow that," Ross said, wiping sweat from his face, "pretty good huh?"

"Yes," I replied, "very impressive bitonal range. Holly wants to have a go but she's too nervous."

"Really?" Ross searched in a jacket pocket and took out a small plastic bag. Peeking inside, he selected a pill and dropped it into Holly's beer. "Drink up," he said.

"What is it? Holly asked.

"Magic," Ross replied, "It will turn you into the best singer in the world. I'm going to have another go while it kicks in. Any requests? No? I might ask denim jacket lady if she wants to do a duet then."

For the record, I should probably note that Holly doesn't usually take drugs. She might have the occasional puff of a joint if offered, but she doesn't smoke crack or inject heroin into her eyeballs. She also doesn't usually throw back drinks containing magic pills. Ross has a way of normalizing drugs though, and he'd taken four himself earlier and hadn't died.

"What the fuck is an island in a stream?" Holly asked, "Do they mean stepping stones?"

"Probably. You feeling all right?"

"Yes, I feel great. Definitely down for a bit of karaoke when these two are done singing about rocks."

Holly's karaoke debut was, well, I've never seen anything like it so I lack an appropriate adjective. Perhaps a combination of the adjectives spectacular, frightening, and energetic. Holly's karaoke debut was spightetic. The regulars at the bar certainly hadn't seen anything quite so spightetic, they've likely not since. Not only did Holly know every word to *No Sleep Till Brooklyn* by the Beastie Boys, she knew all the moves as well. She hipped and hopped and wopped and spighteticized all over the stage, throwing gangsta signs and cold kickin' it live.

Ross missed most of the performance because he was in the bathroom with denim jacket lady, but he caught the tail end where Holly did a Patrick Swayze knee slide across the stage and dropped the mike. The bar was silent for a long moment. Then erupted in applause.

That was pretty much it for Holly, she was now ready to quit her day job and become a professional karaoke singer. She owned the stage until 2am when the bar closed, and ordered a karaoke machine on Amazon at 2.15am. Not just any karaoke machine either, it has a fuckzillion watts, a thirty-foot subwoofer, and laser lights that will take out a retina. It's also portable. This means Holly can take it anywhere. And she does.

"So the funeral is at 1pm, followed by a small gathering of twenty or so people at my house."
"Ooh, should I bring my karaoke machine?"

To: All Staff
From: Jennifer Haines
Date: Friday 20 March 2020 4.06pm
Subject: Quick update

Good afternoon everyone,

Quick update on Dan's 50th. We're expecting around 30 people and the weather should be nice so we're moving the party outside to cater for those who are concerned about social distancing. Masks aren't required but nobody will judge you if you want to wear one. David, please let Holly know that we have an extension cable for her karaoke machine so she doesn't need to bring one. Enjoy your camping trip this weekend.

Gary, Mike has approved you working from home but you can't take your desk and chair. You have to buy your own desk and chair or use a dining table like everyone else if you want to work remotely.

Walter, the Scotts grass seed packaging is due today. I know you were at a lake yesterday so there'd better not be any excuses for it not being done. Also, you sent Erin a photo of a fish. Please double check the recipient's name before clicking send.

Jodie and Melissa, there is no need to keep a tally of each other's toilet paper use. I have removed the chart.

Thank you, Jen

JM showed me his new tent pegs. They were metal with a curve on one end and hardly worth the effort of rummaging through his gear for ten minutes to locate. This was what it had come to though. I'd tried to convince Seb to come to Deer Camp that weekend, it would have meant having someone to ride ATVs with and help fill awkward silences, but he declined citing the lack of social distancing, masks, and unexplored ATV trails. Holly isn't allowed to go to camp because she complains the whole time and asks "When are we leaving?" the moment we wake up the next morning.

"No rush, I'll just start packing stuff up while you drink your coffee."
"Well, no, I can't relax and enjoy my coffee if you're pulling down tent poles behind me, Holly. I'll feel either obligated to help or bad for not helping."
"I'll do it quietly, turn your chair around and face the other way so you can't see me."
"I was actually planning to hang out for a few hours."
"What for?"
"To relax. Maybe ride the ATVs a bit."
"You did that yesterday. If we pack up now and leave within the next thirty minutes, we'll be home in time for my 9am Dance Cardio Zoom workout."

Holly dropped almost three grand on home gym equipment when the pandemic began. She justified the cost by saying it actually saved money on gym membership fees. I've seen the commercials for Planet Fitness so I know membership costs ten dollars a month, which means the equipment will pay for itself in twenty-five years. She actually paid six hundred dollars just for a rowing machine. I could buy an actual boat for less than that. I'm not joking, I looked on Craigslist. Someone is selling a rowboat with two life vests and a fishing rod for three hundred dollars. That's a pretty sweet deal. Holly has been hinting at a Peloton for Christmas but I looked it up and it's two grand plus a monthly subscription. I ordered her a Huffy mountain bike instead - same thing but with fresh air. I also bought her a Rachael Ray nonstick saucepan & skillet set with bonus spatula and egg rings, so someone's getting spoiled this year.

I knew, gazing across the silent campfire at JM and Mark, both staring at their phones, that the conversations wouldn't be censored if I'd stayed at home. They'd be free to giggle like infatuated school girls over photos of Tucker Carlson's hair, high-five each other over the four-inches of new border wall built, and wank each other off while watching video footage of Mitch McConnell's turkey neck flapping about. Perhaps, for the sake of conviviality, I should learn to keep my mouth shut. Trade outrage for trail riding and distaste for companionship. Disappointment is difficult to disguise though. The desire to shake them out of it, to tell them you know they are better than this, is stronger than the desire for amity, and, before you know it, someone is sooking in a tent.

"Oh, don't go to bed, JM. Please stay up and tell us more about government overreach."

Rednecks used to be entertaining. They struck oil and moved to Beverly Hills and jumped cars over creeks. They were good ol' boys, never meanin' no harm. You couldn't pitch television shows like that these days.

"So it's about two rednecks who drive around in an orange car with a confederate flag painted on the roof?"

"Yes, and they have compound bows that shoot arrows with explosives on them."

"Right. Does the car need to have the confederate flag on it?"

"Yes, that's how you know they're rednecks."

"It's just that it's a bit of a touchy subject. We'd be alienating a majority of the American viewing public."

"It's history, not hate."

"Sure. So they just drive around and shoot things with explosive arrows?"

"No, of course not. They have adventures."

"Oh, okay. That sounds fun. What kind of adventures?"

"Beating up faggots and niggers."

"Sorry, what?"

"Foiling bank robberies and saving orphanages."

Rednecks aren't entertaining anymore, they're dangerous. There's a lot of them and they're allowed to vote. The problem with this is that they aren't capable of recognising a grift when they see one. It's why there's a market for country music CD box sets, commemorative coins, bottle openers shaped like bullets, and *Duck Dynasty* apparel.

A few hundred years ago, they'd be the ones gathered around Professor Buttfig's Fixall Elixir Wagon, nodding slack-jawed in amazement as a random audience cripple is invited up on stage, takes a sip of elixir, and throws away his crutches. "It's a miracle!" someone would shout, and Professor Buttfig would shout back, "No, it's science!"

"Will it grow back teefers?"
"Yes."
"Will it cure my Betty Sue's rickets?"
"Of course."
"What about syphilis? Asking for a friend."
"A single sip."
"If I pour it on a dead pig, will it bring it back to life?"
"Um, sure."
"Will it bring back jobs in the coal mining industry?"
"Overnight."

Ideally, there'd be some kind of aptitude test you have to complete before you're allowed to vote. Something that determines whether you're capable of making an educated decision or not. If, for example, you wear a *Duck Dynasty* t-shirt to the test, you're immediately eliminated. Literally, not figuratively. You're taken out back and shot. Stage two of the test, for those not wearing *Duck Dynasty* t-shirts, could consist of being shown a photograph of a reality game show host and being asked if the person in the photo is A. Someone you'd trust with nuclear codes, or B. A deranged clown.

In this region of America at least, you'd need a really big pit out the back. Or perhaps some kind of processing plant that converts the bodies into fertilizer. That way, they'd be of some use to society. Sure, there'd be a shortage of people to work in Dollar General stores and a surplus of chewing tobacco and Wrangler jeans, but things have a way of balancing themselves out. It's like cancer treatment; there's a recovery time and you have to wear a hat for a few months, but the benefits far outweigh the inconvenience. *Dancing With the Stars* would be cancelled. As would *Fox News* and every show about finding Bigfoot. Communities like Elkton* in Virginia would become ghost towns with raised pickup trucks rusting in driveways and domestic violence restraint orders blowing down streets like tumbleweeds. The only negative I can think of is that Denny's would close its doors. Dining at a Denny's may be more depressing than losing a loved one, but they make a decent toasted cheese sandwich. I've no idea where they get bread that thick.

When I was about fifteen, I made myself scrambled eggs on toast. There was nothing special about the scrambled eggs, or the toast, and I'd made the same meal a dozen times. There was something off about the scrambled eggs on toast that day though. Something acrid, something crunchy.

---

* *A ring of meth labs built around a garbage dump. Technically it's a town, but technically Waffle House is a restaurant. Elkton's only export is child molesters.*

Scraping the scrambled eggs away, to get a better look at the toast, I discovered a circular dark spot, about the size of a ten-cent piece, that went all the way through. It was on both pieces of toast, one slightly larger than the other, and I'd eaten half of one of the crunchy acrid spots. I hadn't noticed the dark spots when I put the bread in the toaster, but I hadn't really been paying much attention. Who does?

I retrieved the bag of sliced bread from the cupboard, opened it, and peered inside. The first couple of slices - the crust and second slice - were ones I'd bypassed, as you do, because they're poisonous or something. The third slice had a dark spot, slightly larger than a ten-cent piece, the fourth slice also had one, bigger again. The dark spots weren't as dark as the toasted spots, more of a grey, and you could see more detail - almost like cross sections of a tree. The dark spots grew in size for the next few slices, then started to get smaller again, then a line appeared, spreading out from the dark spot, becoming more defined with each slice.

I was half way through the loaf of bread before I realized it was a moth. Not one of the little "Ew, a moth, get out of here you," type of moths, it was one of the "Jesus fucking Christ, look how big that moth is," type of summer evening moths that sit on your window and stare in and occasionally find their way inside and flap towards you and you almost have a heart attack because you think you're being attacked by a bat.

I'd eaten a cross section of a giant moth's abdomen. Its arse.

Ever since that day, I've held every single slice of bread up to a light to inspect it before toasting it or making a sandwich. One might assume that a moth finding its way into a bakery and being baked into a loaf would be a rare occurrence, but one would be wrong. They bake bread at night.

In the last thirty odd years of holding slices of bread up to a light, I've discovered hundreds of moths. None have been as large as the first moth, but that just makes them harder to see. I've also discovered a cockroach, dozens of mouse droppings, a lady bug, a metal staple, and what I'm pretty sure was the tip of someone's finger. It's not brand specific either, I won't buy Sunbeam at all any more after discovering the cockroach, but Pepperidge Farm, Tip Top, Sara Lee, and even Helga's have their fair share of foreign matter.

The thing is, without holding every slice up to a light, you'd never know. I probably ate hundreds of moths and dozens of mouse droppings before I started checking, and may have missed a few since - gnats and small droppings are hard to tell from grains. Maybe I'd be better off if I'd never discovered the giant moth, just spent my life gobbling down slices of bread blissfully ignorant to the number of moths they hide. Or maybe everyone should hold their slices of bread up to a light and say, "What the fuck, bakeries? This isn't at all acceptable."

Sometimes it would be helpful to be able to hold people up to a light.

The worst part about the current political environment isn't the divisiveness and anger, it's what we've learned about our family and friends. It's like they were replaced by mean pod people, or received an official document stating, "It's okay to be a cunt."

Every few months, a halfwit I know posts the same stupid meme on his Facebook page that consists of two stick figures, a man and a woman, with copy that reads, "This is Bob. He voted for Trump. This is Bob's friend Sally. Sally is a Democrat. Bob and Sally are still friends, because Bob and Sally are adults."

Please. You're the bad guys. You held yourselves up to a light and showed how riddled with moths and mouse shit you are. It's easy to declare, "Having different opinions doesn't mean we can't all get along," but when one opinion is based on decency and common sense, and the other on being an arsehole and refusing to join the dots, it's a bit of a tall ask expecting it to work both ways. It's like Jeffrey Dahmer magnanimously accepting the fact that you're a vegetarian.

"Just try a bit."
"I'm really not hungry, Jeffrey."
"I tried your cauliflower and broccoli cheese crepes."

It's not like Bob and Sally have differing opinions on what they like on their hotdogs or which underarm deodorant works best. Bob's an arsehole and Sally is a coward.

It's actually quite annoying that all of the 'fun' Americans I know are rednecks. They're the ones that ride ATVs and shoot guns and drink bourbon. Not necessarily in that order. None of the 'liberal' Americans I associate with are the slightest bit fun. They're far too busy being offended by everything for frivolous behaviour.

"What have you been up to, Ben?"
"Well, I recently started a petition against large belt buckles. Anything above two inches is simply a display of toxic masculinity. I also started my own Tumblr blog called *Whispered Screams*, a collection of my poetry. Would you like to hear my latest? It's titled *Someone Stole My BLM Sign*."
"No thanks."

Sure, there are times when I'd rather discuss human rights and shrinking ice sheets than the best way to cook squirrel and how to fuck a raccoon without being scratched, but only if the conversation lasts less than five minutes and I don't have to drink beetroot flavoured beer. Perhaps, and this is a distinct possibility, I just hate everyone at the moment. Maybe it's a result of being quarantined for so long; the isolation forcing me to acknowledge who and what I miss, and realising the list isn't as long as it should be. Maybe I'll never leave the house again, just write everyone off and eat a lot of crepes and blame having no pants that fit for not attending social events. Fuck interaction and discourse, I get all the information I need from algorithms customised to generate content sympathetic to my views.

With restaurants and bars closed, and the days getting colder, there's little reason to leave the house anyway. I can see what's happening outside if I need to, our house has windows, but there's not much going on out there.

"I looked out the window this afternoon."
"You did? Anything new?"
"It might be Autumn."

Our neighbours across the street have a cat that stares out of their front window all day. I've never seen the cat outside so I assume it's an interior only one. Like certain paints or cushions that haven't been Scotchgarded. Last week, while I was standing at our front window looking out, I realized the cat and I were doing the same thing. We were like mirror images or goldfish in distant bowls. We stared across the street at each other for a few minutes, then I waved, and I swear the cat waved back. It's possible he was just swiping at a moth or something, or perhaps I experienced a mild form of cabin fever and imagined it. I did have a dream that night about the cat giving me a haircut. It was the best haircut I'd ever had and I remember thinking in my dream, 'I should take a photo of this haircut so I can recreate it,' but then deciding that wasn't neccessary because I'd just get the cat to cut it every time.

It's also possible the cat, caught off guard, waved and then thought, 'Fuck, I'm not meant to interact like that. Stay cool and he'll think I was swiping at a moth or something.'

Recently, I went eight weeks without leaving the house. When I eventually had to, to purchase non-droopy spring onions*, it took me an hour to get dressed, as I had no idea what I used to wear in public, and I had to relearn how to operate a motor vehicle. I blame the gear shifter in my car for the dent in our garage door. Instead of a normal shifter in the console that you move back and forth, I have a round knob on the dashboard, right next to the stereo. It's only a matter of time before I'm doing eighty, attempt to change the music volume, and put the vehicle into reverse.

Thankfully, access to delivery services such as Instacart means I rarely need to leave the house to buy groceries. For those unfamiliar with Instacart, a 'personal shopper' drives to the supermarket, does all your shopping for you, and delivers the groceries to your front door. You then give them an eighty-cent tip and a bad rating through the Instacart app because they selected droopy spring onions.

"What's for dinner?"
"Nothing. The spring onions are droopy."
"Not every meal needs a chopped spring onion sprinkle."
"Of course it does. It's about presentation. Without a spring onion sprinkle, I may as well serve dinner in a bucket. Or just throw it on the floor. Is that how we live now?"

---

* *Spring onions are called 'green onions' in America. The first time I asked a supermarket assistant for spring onions, he said, "It's summer."*

I read somewhere that Facebook has played an integral role in helping people feel connected during the pandemic, but I've unfriended a lot more people than I've friended this year. I'm not a fan of Facebook in general as it mostly consists of people posting stuff they did when I wasn't there. If I wasn't there, I don't give a fuck. If it seems like something I might have enjoyed being there for, fuck you for not inviting me. A photo of your cat? Didn't need to be there. The cat looks like every other cat on the planet. A photo of you drinking beer around a fire pit with a dozen other people I know? I hope someone throws a bag of gunpowder and nails in.

I usually unfriend people the second they post religious quotes, photos of cats, stuff about mistreated dogs, photos of their car, photos of their haircut, photos of them playing frisbee golf, and anything to do with movember, astrology, or fun runs. There's no real rule, it depends on my mood on the day. I unfriended someone this morning because my arm hurt. Yesterday, I unfriended someone because she asked for Netflix recommendations. If I have to scroll endlessly through the Netflix's stupid interface before making a selection, so can everyone else. I'm not Roger Ebert. Having extended the 'unfriend' rule recently to anyone posting pro-Trump or anti-mask political statements, I now have a negative number of friends on Facebook - when I view the list, weird code runs down my screen for a few seconds and then my laptop explodes. For a while I was just clicking the 'unfollow' button, but people you unfollow don't know you've unfollowed them which doesn't send much of a message.

"Did you unfriend me on Facebook?"

"Yes."

"Why?"

"Because I don't like you anymore. I'm not sure that I ever did really. I only accepted your friend request so I could see your photos and they're boring."

"Wow. Thanks, Dad. Having a bad day?"

"Yes, my arm hurts."

Holly has around a thousand 'friends' on her Facebook list but only about ten are actual friends. Sometimes when she posts a photo, someone will comment and I'll ask who that person is and Holly will reply with, "I don't know. I think he was the assistant rep for a company that did subcontract work for a company that used to do the printing for the company that the people who did our flyers used." So it's probably really someone Holly dated before she met me. Why would anyone write, "Looks great!" in response to a post about our new deck unless there was some kind of history there? Keep it in your pants, Todd McNamara.

Dozens of the people on Holly's Facebook friend list are people she currently works with, which means she has to be careful about what she posts. A lot of them are rednecks from neighbouring towns like Elkton, so she can't post anything about my website or books in case her coworkers discover I've written something unflattering about them. Especially Stephanie who looks like a gnome with Down syndrome.

Stephanie is the IT manager at the community bank Holly works for. She gave herself that title because she owns an Apple Watch. She also runs her own 'catering business' from her home kitchen, which means every work function has beans, macaroni & cheese, and some kind of stringy meat, possibly roadkill, on the menu. It's sixteen different flavours of hell but Stephanie would have a major melt-down if anyone suggested using a real caterer. I don't eat anything at the work functions because I'm not a fan of cat hair and salmonella poisoning.

"Whatcha' cookin', Momma?"
"Beans, mac & cheese, and some kind of stringy meat."
"Can I help?"
"Sure, the mac & cheese is a bit dry so you can add some milk."
"We're out of milk."
"Hold Snowy over the pot and squeeze a teat. She's just had kittens."

It's easy to be critical. Real easy. Stephanie's gastroenteritis chafers aren't the worst thing I've ever tasted though. That honour belongs to Holly's homemade kombucha. I'd never even heard of kombucha until she bought a DIY kit and turned our kitchen into a laboratory. For three weeks, a huge jellyfish-shaped blob of bacteria sat fermenting in a five-gallon jug of tea on our countertop. Even just looking at the blob made me feel ill - the one time I had a curious sniff, I dry-retched for about three minutes and had to lie down.

Tasting the terrifying slop wasn't by choice; Holly made tacos one night and added a hot sauce she'd ordered online called Da Bomb Beyond Insanity. I'm not sure what the Scoville rating of the sauce is, I doubt Mr Scoville even had this kind of bullshit in mind when he came up with the chart. I've been on actual fire before and that was nowhere near as painful. This was like being kicked in the face by a horse made out of fire-ants and the worst thing I'd ever put in my mouth - up until I grabbed Holly's glass of what I thought was apple juice and threw it back. It's impossible to describe the taste of Holly's homemade kombucha, it was all the tastes, but a blend of vinegar, fish, whiteboard cleaner, brake fluid, and magnets comes close.

"I'm going blind."

"Please, you're overreacting a bit."

"It's the worst thing I've ever tasted and I once ate a moth. My face is melting and now I've been poisoned."

"Here, drink this glass of milk, it'll cool your mouth."

"Did you use the same glass the kombucha was in?"

"I rinsed it first."

"No you didn't."

"How can you tell?"

"The milk's curdled. It's like a sloppy cheese."

I caught Holly pouring the jug of kombucha down the sink a few hours later. I nodded and said, "Pretty bad, huh?" and she replied, "No, it was quite good but I found a dead millipede in the jug. I'll cover it with cheesecloth next time."

Also, before Holly poured the jug down the sink, she took a photo and posted it on Facebook with the hashtags #firsttryatkombucha #turnedoutamazing #yum. Stephanie commented, "You'll have to give me the recipe!" so I replied with, "Do you have any millipedes?" and Holly deleted my comment and yelled at me.

I was blocked from commenting on Holly's Facebook page for a while. "Just until I can trust you." I was also told I'm not going to her next work function, so some good came of it. Holly's work functions are like clubhouse meetings for village idiots. Village idiots devoid of any personality, social skills, or fashion sense. The men all wear grey polyester double-breasted suits two sizes too large for them, and the women all wear polyester floral dresses from the grandma department at J. C. Penney. If a fire broke out, they'd all melt together into a huge conglomerate of sadness. At least that would be some excitement though.

"And what do you do, David?"
"Workwise? I trick people into purchasing products they don't need by making the box they come in look nice. What do you do, Harold?"
"I'm an investment banking associate. It's very interesting work actually. I identify and meet clients' financial goals by creating valuation models, specifically LBO, DCF and accretion/dilution analysis…oh no, the building is on fire, we're all going to die."
"Thank Christ. I hope it's quick."

Holly's work Christmas parties are the worst. The dictionary defines a party as a group of people taking part in a particular activity, so I guess using the word party is technically correct, but that's where the similarity ends. Everyone just shuffles around aimlessly, holding their two drink tickets, occasionally forming small groups where they stand and nod for several minutes before moving on. It's dreadful and I wouldn't wish the experience on anyone.

"You talk funny."

"Yes, that's probably the Australian accent."

"Are you from Australia?"

"No, Norway. I just put on an Australian accent because the Norwegian accent is dreadful. It's like speaking German after being kicked in the groin. What do you do, Jordan?"

"I'm a commercial loan officer."

"If I ask what that entails will your answer take longer than five seconds?"

"Yes."

"Well it was nice meeting you. Cool sweater by the way."

Who wears a *Make Christmas Great Again* sweater to an office Christmas party? I get that it's the festive version of the red cap, and that it saves people the trouble of talking to you to realize you're a halfwit, but you couldn't go one night without being a dick? Jordan and his hideous bug-eyed redheaded wife probably thought it was the most hilarious thing they'd seen since that episode of *Friends* where Phoebe sang *Smelly Cat*.

The most interesting person that Holly works with is a deaf guy that wears wacky socks to work.

"Oh my god, have you seen Ken's socks today? They have billiard balls on them. He's such a card. He should be doing stand-up instead of debt consolidation."

I have nothing against deaf people but the 'nuhugghnnn' noise gets a bit annoying and there's no point trying to teach me to say banana with hand movements that look like you're conjuring a water demon because I'm not going to remember it. Just carry a pad and pencil around and either write the word banana or draw one. Also, the jazz fingers instead of clapping thing. Not a huge fan. I once worked with a deaf guy named Neil. He looked like a human/axolotl hybrid and had red hair so there wasn't a lot going for him. We worked in different departments - he was an account rep while I was in the art department - but we often had to drive to client meetings together. The trips were excruciating because he drove a manual hatchback and, even at highway speeds, never went above second gear. The engine screamed and the RPM gauge redlined while he sat there oblivious. Sometimes I'd try to alert him to the fact but he'd just smile and nod and say, "Nuhugghnnn." We were late for a meeting one afternoon and, after gunning his vehicle harder than usual, the engine blew up. Cylinders actually punched through the hood and flames came out the air-conditioning vents. Also, if you can't hear people knocking on your office door, perhaps lock it if you're planning on having a lunch wank.

Holly and I have talked about moving, but I'm sure there are slack-jawed inbreds in every city and town throughout America. Maybe it's just a matter of working out the ratio of slack jawed inbreds to normal humans. Where we currently live, the ratio is about seventy-thirty, so I guess anywhere a bit more balanced would be preferable. Boulder, Colorado looks nice. It has a lot of trees and marijuana is legalized. That would save having to pretend I like my dealer Andrew. Seattle is also nice but real estate prices there are kind of ridiculous.

"So it's a cardboard box on the side of a street?"
"Yes, but check out the view. Location, location, location."
"And they're asking how much?"
"It's listed at six-hundred-thousand but there may be some wriggle room as the seller is motivated."
"What about HOA fees?"
"Four-hundred per week but that includes use of the pool."
"There's a pool?"
"Technically it's a puddle but it's yours to use whenever you like. When it rains. Which is quite often. That's why the box has a tarp over it."

We plan to visit Boulder next year if the pandemic is under control by then. We've already visited several cities in several states and they've all been shitholes so we crossed them off our list. You couldn't pay me to live in LA, or any city in Florida, and I'd rather be dead than live in New Orleans. There's only so much jazz music I can handle and it's none.

To: All Staff
From: Jennifer Haines
Date: Tuesday 24 March 2020 9.19am
Subject: Dan's birthday update

Good morning,

Just letting everyone know we may need to postpone Dan's birthday party. He's still overseas at the moment and having difficulty with flights so he might not be back in time. Please check your calendars.

Cara's school cancelled classes so I'll be working remotely from home for a few weeks. Gary, Rebecca and Jodie are now working remotely so Melissa will be holding the fort for the moment. Yes, it's inconvenient for everyone but hopefully this Covid thing won't drag on much longer.

Walter, please send Ben ALL emails to proofread before you send them to clients. You wrote "I'm happy 2 be helicopter" in your last email to Erin instead of, "happy to be helpful." Also, please don't use numbers in place of words and please change your email signature to the approved text, you can't use a photo of your mountain bike.

Please note: I'll be in the office for all weekly production meetings. We can use Zoom for those who choose not to attend in person but it would be nice if everyone at least tried to make the effort. It's not the end of the world people.

Thank you, Jen

I have actually put on a couple of cats since the pandemic began. People used to say to me, "You're way too skinny, David, eat a block of cheese or something," and I was quite self-conscious of my scrawny frame when I was in my teens. I avoided any environment where I would have to take my shirt off in public, such as the beach or swimming pools, and I forged dozens of notes to get out of showering at gym in high school.

"David, this note states you have smallpox."
"Yes. Just on my chest though, that's why I can't take my shirt off."
"Smallpox was eradicated in the early nineteen hundreds."
"It's a different type of smallpox. Smallerpox."
"Right. Last week you had rabies."
"Yes, a bat bit my chest."

I did make a concerted effort to gain weight when I was twelve. I collected comics back then and one had an advertisement on the back for a body building course by Charles Atlas. It guaranteed 'a big chest, powerful legs, strong arms, success with girls, and a magnetic personality' in just seven days for two dollars. I filled in my address details, cut out the advertisement, and mailed it - with an Australian two-dollar note included - to the United States address listed. A year later, I received a booklet that advises the reader to get enough sleep, exercise regularly, keep a positive attitude, and listen to good music. I also tried eating copious amounts of everything on the pointy bit of the food pyramid for two weeks, but my metabolism must have been quicker than my calorie intake. It was also around the time I discovered masturbation so I was probably inadvertently working off all the extra sugar and bread.

"Where's David?"
"Taking a shower."
"Again? Who takes six or seven showers a day? Our water heater isn't big enough for that."
"He said he was sweaty."

My father actually had very strict water usage rules when I was growing up. If using the sink, under no circumstances were we to use the hot tap. If using the shower, we were not to exceed three minutes. He would set a timer and if the water was still on when the buzzer went off, he'd barge into the bathroom yelling and turn it off. He was a bit of a dick. As the shower took a few minutes to warm up, I had to lather myself with soap and shampoo outside the stream and use the remaining sixty seconds to wash it off.

After my father ran off with the lady that did the member's fees and match scheduling at his tennis club, I took as long as I wanted in the shower. Since then, my showers have extended to two, sometimes three, hours. I usually turn on the shower and make a coffee while waiting for it to get nice and steamy. Then I get in and have my coffee with a cigarette. After enjoying the water for a while, I shave, brush my teeth, shampoo my hair and wash. In that order but the time between each varies. Then I enjoy the water for a while. Sometimes I'll try to drown a bug or see how much water I can hold with my arms crossed, or hold my arms down with my fingers splayed to make the water run off the tips. My current bathroom has a television and coffee machine in it. I tried putting a beanbag in the shower but, after a few months, the stitching rotted away and it burst so now I use a camping chair.

People don't talk about 'skinny shaming', I'm not sure it's even a term, but kids are arseholes and being six foot and weighing only two buckets of water in eighth grade means you stand out as an easy target. My nickname for a while was 'Muntabi' because of a television commercial for WorldVision featuring a skinny black kid with a voice over stating, "Muntabi was abandoned by his parents and hasn't eaten in two weeks." After watching a David Attenborough documentary on insects during biology class, my nickname was changed to 'Stick Insect', which was eventually shortened to 'Sticky'.

I hated the nickname a lot more than I let on. Kids would yell, "Hey Sticky, do the walk!" and I'd walk in slow motion with exaggerated hand and leg motions to show I found the whole thing hilarious and wasn't bothered by the name one bit. Thankfully, after a falling out with my best friend Michael over skateboard wheels, or perhaps the bearings, he told everyone at school I wanked off a dog and my nickname was changed to Dogtosser.

It could have been worse, there was a boy in our class named Leslie Bean. If you name a male child Leslie, you're effectively setting him up to be ridiculed. The only name worse is Gaylord.

"We should name him Leslie."
"Really?"
"What's wrong with the name Leslie?"
"It's a girl's name. A fat British girl's name."
"No it isn't, it's spelled completely differently."
"Yes, but it sounds the same."
"Fine. How about Gaylord?"
"Leslie it is."

Leslie Bean's original nickname at school was Beanbag until some genius worked out that if you said his first and last name really fast, it sounded a bit like 'lesbian'. Which was doubly clever being that Leslie is a girl's name. There was also a boy in our class named Peter Phillips who kids called Pedophile Lips for a while, but it was a bit of a mouthful so never stuck and was eventually changed to Wobble because of the way he walked. I think he had spina bifada.

Leslie was forced to endure daily comments such as, "Kissed any girls lately, Lesbian?" Which isn't much of an insult but it seemed to get under Leslie's skin. He went to the principal's office to complain about being called Lesbian and the principal spoke about it during that week's assembly, which effectively formalized the nickname.

During history class one afternoon, our teacher, Mr Stobie, had to leave the class for fifteen minutes and told us to read quietly while he was gone. Kids don't read quietly when the teacher leaves the class, it becomes a condensed version of *Lord of the Flies*. Factions are formed, wars break out, the weak are preyed upon. If left unsupervised for long enough, a dictatorial government forms and dissenters are put to death. For some reason, it was 'a thing' in our class that whenever we were left unsupervised, someone's pencil case was grabbed and thrown into a ceiling fan. The pencil case would explode and the contents would be strewn about the room. I'd had my pencil case 'fanned' a couple of times and it was pretty annoying as you had to crawl around the floor and under desks to pick everything up. On this particular afternoon, it was Emma Jenkins' pencil case that exploded, sending pencils, rulers, and erasers flying everywhere. There was also a tube of lipstick.

"Don't let Lesbian get the lipstick," yelled a fat kid named George, "He'll steal it and wear it."

The class laughed. Encouraged by the positive reaction to his incredibly clever comment, George took it further. Pulling back Leslie's chair, causing Leslie to fall to the floor, George straddled Leslie's chest and used his knees to pin down Leslie's arms. Leslie struggled but was no match for George's weight.

"Give me the lipstick," George said to Emma.

It's as if there's a factory that churns out bullies. They're all the same portly short haired yobs. George was fatter than the standard factory edition but apart from that he was stock. He was the kind of kid who would kick a soccer ball at your head or throw your schoolbag into the creek for no other reason than, I suppose, to be the one dishing out hurt rather than taking it. I was once targeted by him for an entire week, I have no idea why, and he made my life a living hell. He put dog poo in my locker, poster paint in my hair, and flushed my *Karate Kid* head bandana down a toilet.

Yes, I wore a bandana to school after seeing the movie.
No, it wasn't a great idea.

I was pretty upset about the bandana; I'd bought it with my own money and had decided it was how I was going to roll from that day forward - I'd be 'David, that kid that looks like the Karate Kid'. I told my mother that evening that George had flushed my bandana - I may have had tears in my eyes - and she said, "Have you tried being friends with him?"

How the fuck does that help anyone? A week or so later, when my mother was upset over an argument with the lady next door about cutting down an azalea bush, I asked, "Have you tried being friends with her?" and was told not to be so fucking stupid. So there's your answer; it doesn't help anyone. Get on the phone, ring George's mother, and demand that she purchases a replacement *Karate Kid* bandana within the next 24 hours or you'll ring the police.

"Where's Leslie?" asked Mr Stobie, sitting down at his desk.

He was met with silence.

"Did he go to the bathroom?"

"He went shopping for a dress," George quipped.

There was a smattering of nervous laughter.

"Yes, hilarious, George," said Mr Stobie. "You know, if you spent as much time jogging as you do seeking attention, you wouldn't be such a fat cunt."

These days, if a teacher body shames a student, it's all over the media, the teacher loses their position, and the school is likely sued. It was like the Wild West in Australian schools during the eighties - minus the hats, horses, and death by dysentery. Teachers slapped you on the back of the head as they walked between desks, smoked in class, called boys Nancys and Poofters if they weren't good at sports, and used the B word* to describe Aboriginal students. Just a few years before, teachers were allowed to cane students so perhaps, robbed of the power to physically scar children, they were lashing out in the only way they had left. Once, Mr Stobie told me I looked like a child's stick-figure drawing. Another time, he told me that my parents should have aborted me because I couldn't find Poland on a map. Who the fuck knows where Poland is on a map?

---

* Boong. An offensive Australian ethnic pejorative or slur for Aboriginals, similar to using the N word. Derived from the sound Aboriginals make when they bounce off the front of a vehicle at high speed.

will just have to give his presentation
. Next on the list is... Mister Thorne. This
.ting. Have you completed the assignment,

ie."
"Vv ι_   rs never cease. And which historic war or battle
did you choose to write about?"
"The Battle of Hoth."
"Hmm. I don't believe I'm familiar with that battle. Please
continue."
"A long time ago, in a galaxy far, far away..."
"Sit down. No, actually, sit outside. I don't want to see your
face again today."
"It's raining."
"Good. With any luck, you'll catch pneumonia and die.
Nobody will miss you. Okay, next up is... Allison. Have you
completed the assignment, Allison?"
"No."
"Of course you haven't, you toothless halfwit. You know,
I met your parents at last week's parent-teacher night and it
was patently obvious they're siblings."

Mr Stobie was eventually fired. Not for calling kids fat cunts
or inbreds, for being inebriated at school. He backed over
Toby the wheelchair kid in the teacher's parking lot with his
station wagon and failed a mandatory sobriety test. Toby was
fine. His left leg was broken but it didn't work anyway so I'm
not sure how they knew or why they bothered putting it in
a cast. We all signed his cast regardless and our substitute

history teacher wrote, "You'll be up and about in no time!" on it because she didn't realise Toby was in a wheelchair before the accident.

Leslie didn't return to class. He came to school the next day though. George was sitting on a bench during lunch period, eating a bag of chips, when Leslie walked up behind him, plunged a steak knife into his neck, and casually walked away.

The knife didn't go all the way in, there was an inch or so of blade still showing, and there was surprisingly little blood until George stood and pulled the blade out. There was a lot of screaming - from other kids, not George, his screams were bubbly and barely audible. A teacher on yard duty bolted over in panic and placed her hand on George's neck - which was now squirting a thin but steady fountain of blood.

I was standing less than ten feet away, frozen, I assume in shock at what I was witnessing. Barely thirty seconds before, I'd been approaching George to ask if I could have a chip.

"Give me your t-shirt!" the teacher yelled.
"What?" I asked.
"Take off your t-shirt," she demanded, "I need something to stop the bleeding with."
"No," I said, "I have chest scabies. I have a note."

George died.

No, he was fine. His neck fat saved him. He scored a couple of weeks off school and cool stitches and actually lost a bit of weight from not being able to eat solid foods for a few months. He continued to lose weight, went through an Adam & the Ants phase, and even modelled activewear for a K-Mart catalogue before losing an eye.

To 'turn' a piece of wood on a lathe, you use something called a chuck key - essentially a metal ratchet with handles - to tighten the jaws of a chuck, which holds a block of wood securely. You then *ensure the chuck key is removed* and press a big yellow button. This spins the chuck, along with the block of wood held in its jaws, at horrendous speeds.

While demonstrating how to operate the lathe to a group of students, including myself and George, our shop teacher, Mr Williams, forgot to remove the chuck key.

Afterwards, a few kids swore they had seen a blur as the chuck key left the chuck, but I was watching pretty closely and didn't see anything. George's head was thrown back as if he had been kicked by a horse. His feet actually left the ground. As we stared in horror, George climbed to his feet with a confused look on his face and put his hand up to his eye. Only the chuck-key's handle was visible.

Everybody yelled at the same time. Completely unaware of what was happening due to the noise of the lathe, Mr Williams continued his demonstration.

"Keep the chisel edge at a low angle... "

"MR WILLIAMS!"

"...otherwise it might grab. We don't want any accidents. As you can see, by applying pressure to only the areas you want removed, the candlestick holder begins to take shape."

Mr Williams was placed on leave and didn't come back. George returned after a month or so, but left again after his parents received a large settlement and enrolled him in a private school. He actually went on to take up archery and competed in the 2001 Special Olympics World Games, placing second for a silver medal. The person who took home gold only had missing legs, which seems a bit unfair. They should probably have given George a chair and made the guy in a wheelchair wear an eye patch.

I lost sight in my left eye once. It was only for a few minutes after accidently jabbing myself with a drinking straw while driving, but I know what it's like to live with a disability.

Leslie was expelled from school and the police were involved so I guess he was charged with assault. He probably had to go to a special school for wayward boys or something. I saw him a year or two later while I was on a bus and he was wearing a black t-shirt so I guess he'd decided to embrace the whole bad boy thing. I'd once picked out a black t-shirt while I was shopping for clothes with my mother and was told to put it back because, "Only burglars, gang members, and rapists wear black t-shirts."

Some of the kids in our class were interviewed by police officers about the lipstick incident, but I wasn't one of them. The stabbing made the local news and two girls that hadn't even been in the area when the attack happened were interviewed by a reporter. One of them, a lying trollop named Vicky Chapman, said she had witnessed the whole thing, that it was really sad, and that everyone should just be nice to each other. Bitch, you called me Dogtosser for four years.

After her appearance on the news, Vicky acted like she was a famous award-winning actress and steered all conversation towards her five seconds of fame. She even ran for class president a short time later and wrote 'As seen on TV' on her posters. The posters also said 'Vote Vicky - I'm the missing piece!' with her face on a big jigsaw piece for no fathomable reason.

She lost the election to Helen Roberts who promised longer recess and lunch breaks, monthly class discos, and a slap bracelet for everyone who voted for her. Vicky blamed her loss on bribery and the fact that someone had vandalized almost all of the two hundred posters she put up around the school by adding a unibrow and changing the word 'piece' to 'link'.

"Have you seen Vicky's posters? I wonder who did it. Vicky thinks it was Helen."
"Yes, Helen seems the most likely suspect."

The vandalism, and possibly losing by 4 votes to 178, must have pushed Vicky over the edge because a few days later, Vicky and one of her friends, a huge heifer named Louise*, attacked Helen in the girl's toilets. After forcing Helen into a stall, Louise held the door shut while Vicky urinated into a Slurpee cup and poured it over the top. I felt bad for Helen, and partly responsible, as she ran an honest campaign - even if she didn't have enough slap bracelets for everyone and extended recess and lunch breaks were never really on the table. We did get a class disco though. It was just once, for thirty minutes, during recess in the media room with the blinds closed and a cassingle of *Hold Me Now* by the Thompson Twins played on loop, but promises made, promises kept.

Vicky and Louise were suspended for a week, which seems a light punishment in hindsight, but they also had to apologise to Helen during assembly in front of the whole school, which must have been horrible. Vicky also bore the nickname 'Link' for almost a year until she became pregnant at fourteen and it was changed to 'Preggers'. There was a rumour going around for a while that the father was Toby the wheelchair kid, but I suspect it may have been Toby who started it.

---

* *Louise had tight curly hair and a moustache. Once during a school game of soccer, she ran to the edge of the playing field, dropped her shorts, and did a poo. This is the kind of thing people named Louise do. The gym teacher had to pick it up with a plastic shopping bag.*

That was all way back when schoolyard bullying was still a thing of course. It's not like that anymore. In 2018, the First Lady of the United States, Melanoma Trump, initiated a public awareness campaign to combat bullying called *Be Best*. Within days of its launch, all bullying, worldwide, ceased to exist.

"Nice pants, retard."
"Be best."
"I apologise. My remark was both hurtful and politically incorrect. Will you be my friend?"
"Yes."

Also, just in case you were wondering about Vicky's baby, it was a boy. She named him Tom, after Johnny Depp's character on *21 Jump Street*, and he became a fixture at the school. This was before schools had daycare facilities and Vicky's parents worked, so I guess the only options Vicky had were to leave school or bring Tom to class. He was pretty quiet for the most part and Vicky constantly forgot he was there. Once he sat in his stroller in the middle of the school soccer field for three hours, another time he was left on a bus. Tom turned out fine though, I saw him and Vicky in a supermarket fifteen years later and said hello. I learned Tom was working as an apprentice carpenter and that Vicky is incapable of letting go of a grudge. When I brought up the whole 'I'm the missing link' thing, and admitted to being the saboteur, she threw a packet of baby carrots at me and Tom called me a skinny cunt.

To: All Staff
From: Jennifer Haines
Date: Monday 30 March 2020 1.53pm
Subject: Dan's party postponed

Good afternoon everyone,

Sadly, Dan's party is now officially postponed. Please check your calendars. Dan managed to get flights but he won't be home until the 8th. We plan to reschedule for the following month so don't pack away those party dresses just yet.

In happier news, I'm sure everyone will join me in congratulating Melissa and Andrew on their engagement. Yay! From what I've heard, the proposal was very romantic. I couldn't be happier for you both and look forward to receiving a wedding invite. <3

Jodie, please keep your comments and innuendos about scouts and scoutmasters to yourself. We've heard them all and they're not funny.

Everyone, please check your calendars and have Zoom set up and working for our first online production meeting this Friday. David will email step by step instructions this afternoon seeing as a few people are having trouble. Gary, you need to take the strip of tape off your camera for everyone to see you. You can put it back on after the meeting but nobody is spying on you.

Thank you, Jen

Scoutmaster Andrew's proposal to Melissa *was* actually annoyingly romantic. He took her camping to his favourite spot, by a river in the George Washington National Forest, but had driven to the campsite earlier that morning and set up fairy lights and a table with white linen and champagne on ice as a surprise.

I proposed to Holly while we were playing tennis and she's never let me forget it. Whenever anyone describes the romantic situation in which they were proposed to, Holly gives me a pursed lip glance. If I could go back in time, I'd at least let her win the match. It's gotten to the point where Holly actually blatantly lies about the proposal.

"And then, as Jeff and I watched the sun set in Bora Bora, the waiter brought me a piña colada and the ring was around the straw. How did David propose to you?"

"He wrote, "Holly, will you marry me?" in fireworks."

"Really?"

"Yes. And there was a band playing."

"Gosh, who?"

"The Beastie Boys."

"Oh my lord, where was it?"

"On the moon. David hired a rocket to take us all there. The fireworks people had to write, "Holly, will you marry me?" backwards because we were looking down at the Earth instead of up from it."

"You've been to the moon?"

"Yes, and the sun."

Even if I had thought to do something more romantic, I didn't have the kind of money back then that words written in fireworks probably cost. I had quit my job, sold everything I owned, moved countries, and leased a two-bedroom A-frame in a small ski-resort in Virginia. The A-frame was built in 1957 and had only been renovated once since - in 1972. It had blue shag-pile carpet, even in the bathroom and kitchen, and orange Formica countertops. The back wall consisted entirely of large glass windows looking out onto a forest, which was nice, but, during winter, anything within six feet of the windows froze solid. During summer, the same six feet became another dimension. A wavy dimension with mirages. Anyone entering the heat zone was instantly mummified and a ficus actually caught fire. There were mushrooms growing in the bathroom, bees living in the attic, and the washing machine, a Westinghouse Washomatic the size of a flexographic printing press, shook the house violently enough for tiles to fall off the kitchen backsplash. I didn't care though, because I was with Holly.

Sure, there are ways to be romantic without spending money, but nobody's really impressed by your shitty picnic or arboretum bridge proposal. I thought tennis was appropriate because it's something Holly and I enjoy doing together. Maybe I should have had a table with white linen and champagne on ice waiting on the court, or maybe written, "Holly will you marry me?" in tennis balls. I didn't though, so there's no point harping on about it. I only had maybe ten tennis balls anyway. Sorry I'm not a coach.

I did buy matching Cartier Love Rings for our tenth anniversary this year - to replace the tin wedding bands we bought when we got married - so that was fairly romantic and, as an added bonus, required minimal effort. We also had flights booked for a week in Japan but our flights were cancelled due to the pandemic. I was quietly happy about this because I'm not a huge fan of flying or vacations. Holly and I have a ritual when we go away; I complain about everything and then we have an argument. Once we land and get to the hotel, I'll declare the hotel is a shithole and that I hate whatever country or city we are in. After that, I get badly sunburnt. By the third or fourth day I'm fine and we go out shopping for a fridge magnet. Then we leave the next day on a 3AM flight.

While Holly and I were on our honeymoon in Mexico, I got so sunburned I had to go to hospital. You don't want to go to a Mexican hospital; everyone yells and old ladies try to sell you roses. Someone at the hospital stole my iPhone and a nurse called me 'estúpido hombre langosta' - which translates to 'stupid lobster man'. I blame Holly entirely for my sunburn; if she hadn't made me paddleboard, I wouldn't have lost my glasses, and wouldn't have sprayed myself all over liberally with a travel-sized can of dry shampoo.

"What the fuck is dry shampoo? And why does it have a picture of a banana on it?"
"That's not a banana, it's a lady's face with flowing yellow hair."

I'm not even sure why paddleboards are a thing. It's not relaxing, you can't drink a beer while doing it, and you look like an idiot. Just sit down. Nobody cares that you have good balance, it's essentially the same skill as standing on a wobbly stool and nobody's calling that a sport. It's like an uncomfortable and unstable version of kayaking for people with hemorrhoids. The person who invented it, probably someone who wears a lot of Prana, should have been told to stop fucking about and sit down.

"Stop fucking about and sit down. You'll hurt yourself."
"No I won't, I have really good balance."
"Nobody cares. What's the point?"
"The point is that I'm standing up. Look at me!"
"You don't look very stable."
"I'm not."
"Or comfortable."
"No."
"You'd be better off in a kayak. They have a seat with a lower center of gravity and paddles that have blades on both ends so you can row faster."
"It's not about speed. It's about standing up. I'm going to call it the Stand Up and Paddle Board."
"So it's just a water version of your other inventions, the Stand Up and Drive Car, the Stand Up and Sleep Bed, and the Stand Up and Wobble Stool?"
"Yes, but I have good feeling about this one."
"That's what you said about the Stand Up and Defecate Toilet and the Stand Up and Roll Wheelchair."

Although I'm not a huge fan of flying or vacations, I have actually missed being able to go anywhere this year due to the pandemic. Perhaps it's a case of wanting the things you can't have. Like the mechanical owl from *Jason and the Argonauts* or gills. Having gills would be fun; if you were at a lake you could dive underwater and hang around for a bit and then when everyone is panicking and thinking you've drowned, you could pop up and say, "Here I am." It would only work once or twice but by that time the novelty of having gills would probably have worn off anyway. It also wouldn't work in really clear water, as everyone would be able to see you and would likely point and ask, "What the fuck is he doing?"

While Holly and I haven't been able to fly anywhere for a vacation, Smith Mountain Lake is an easy drive from where we live. It's a large man-made lake with plenty of pull-up restaurants and quiet coves to anchor in. We have a boat docked at a marina there and before you state, "Well la-di-da, someone owns a boat," our boat is twenty years old and held together by duct tape and mildew. It does have a bed and small galley though, which means we can take the boat out during summer and spend the night anchored in a cove as a kind of mini-getaway. The boat, named Bushpig 2, is actually our second boat. Bushpig 1 sank a few years ago after I forgot to screw the drain plug in. Thankfully the insurance company didn't question how it was possible for a drain plug to 'wiggle itself out' and we purchased Bushpig 2 less than a month later.

Prior to buying a boat, Holly and I had rented a houseboat on Smith Mountain Lake several times. Houseboats are convenient but they're essentially floating trailer homes and are incredibly slow. I've seen paddling ducks overtake us. If you're anchored in a cove and decide to head to a restaurant for lunch, you need to be up around four in the morning and on your way by five. Often, while we were chugging along, boats would zoom past us, towing wakeboarders or tubes with screaming kids in them, and Holly would sigh and say, "That looks like fun."

For the first summer of boat ownership, we took the boat out almost every weekend. We'd wave to other boat owners as we passed as if to say, "Hello fellow boat owners, lovely day on the lake, isn't it?" and they'd wave back. It was all very cordial and everyone was there for the same purpose: to enjoy and share the lake. It was an escape. From work, from worries, from politics. Then, this summer, *Trump 2020* flags began appearing on boats. Big ones flown from the stern. There were even parades where dozens of flag waving rednecks cruised up and down the lake in packs, playing loud songs about eagles and trucks and generally being dickheads. "Where's your Trump flag?" they'd yell as we passed, and I'd yell back, "Where's your teeth?"

Having gills would be fun; if you were at a lake and someone was anchored in a cove with a *Trump 2020* flag waving from the back of their boat, you could swim over to it underwater and unscrew the drain plug.

To: All Staff
From: Jennifer Haines
Date: Thursday 2 April 2020 12.32pm
Subject: Thank you!

Good afternoon everyone,

Dan said to say thank you for the birthday present. It was very nice of you all and completely unexpected. I sent him a photo and he said he's wanted a robotic lawnmower ever since he saw Mike's.

Looking forward to seeing all your faces in tomorrow's Zoom meeting. I love seeing your Facebook posts but it's not the same. David, your deck extension is looking great. You and Seb have certainly been busy. Rebecca, your new bathroom looks beautiful. Walter, I know you blocked me.

Starting Monday, Melissa will be working remotely but she will be going into the office every few days to collect mail etc. The phones will be diverted and Mike is writing an email to send to clients. Melissa, the plants in the boardroom are plastic and don't need to be watered.

Gary, Melissa has a spare key to your office so if you thought we wouldn't notice the missing chair, you were mistaken. Mike said to let you know that the Herman Miller chair is worth more than your car and he expects it to be returned immediately.

Thank you, Jen

The robotic lawnmower *was* actually Mikes. He used it only twice then put it back in the box after Duncan - Mike and Patrick's Yorkshire Terrier - attacked the mower while it was operating and lost a paw. Not all of the paw, just the pad and toes, but Duncan has a weird nub now that makes me feel ill when I look at it.

"Look who's come to visit the office. It's Duncan! Yes it is! Say hello to David, Duncan. Can you shake hands?"
"It's fine, really, he doesn't need to do that."

Holly and I once dogsat Duncan when Mike & Patrick went to Paris for a week. I taped a sock over Duncan's nub on the second day because he kept touching me with it. Every time Mike requested a photo of Duncan, I had to take the shot from the chest up like a fat girl's Facebook profile photo. The first few shots were of Duncan watching television, playing with fluffy toys, and sleeping on the sofa. By the tenth request, I was Photoshopping Duncan onto the roof of our house and jumping through fire pit flames. Mike rang demanding to speak to him twice.

"Hold the phone up to his ear... Hello, Duncan, it's Daddy."
"Woof."
"That was just you saying woof."
"No it wasn't."
"Right, send me a photo of Duncan with a newspaper showing today's date or I'm going to ask Jen to drive to your house and check on him."

Jennifer and Dan couldn't look after Duncan because their house doesn't have a fence around it. I'm not kidding, there's no fence at all; their yard just sort of merges with the neighbour's yard. It's fairly common in America but that doesn't make it any less weird. Sometimes there's whole blocks of houses without fences and the backyards all merge into one giant backyard. The owners only mow their bit though, they're not mowing the whole lot. It probably means having to mow your bit regularly, or your bit will be the only bit that isn't mowed. As such, the robotic mower was probably a handy present but I'm not sure how it's meant to know which bit is Jennifer and Dan's bit or if it just wanders off. Not having a fence is unheard of in Australia, it would be an open invitation for people to take your stuff.

"Look, that house has no fence."
"Does that mean the stuff outside is ours?"
"Yes, I guess it does. You grab our deck furniture and I'll unscrew our hose fittings."

Even fences won't stop your stuff from being nicked in Australia. Jumping a fence and taking things from your neighbour's yard is a generally accepted practice known as 'Snow Dropping'. While the term covers potted plants, hose fittings, and garden furniture, it mainly refers to clothing. Due to the warm climate, most Australians hang their washing outside on a clothesline to dry. This cuts down on the costs of running a dryer and the savings can be put towards purchasing new clothes when you find yours

116

missing. It's not uncommon to be driving through your suburb a few days later and see a neighbour mowing his lawn in your favourite jeans and t-shirt. With your lawn-mower.

"Is that my lawn mower, Barry?"
"Maybe."
"You rascal. I'll be over tonight to get it back."

I'm not sure why it's called Snow Dropping but giving a cute sounding name to a shitty act somehow makes it more acceptable. A copywriter probably came up with it.

"We also need to replace the term 'child molestation'. It sounds a bit, I don't know, molesty."
"How about Snuggle Booping?"
"Perfect."

The last house that Holly and I lived in didn't have a fence but that was because it was a large forested property out in the middle of nowhere. We only had one neighbour, a wrinkly old dickhead named Carl, who mowed his lawn twice a day, yelled a lot, and murdered squirrels for fun. We loved the property but didn't love Carl. It was the first house that Holly and I bought together and I still resent Carl for ruining the whole experience. Every so often, I check the local obituaries to see if he's dead yet...

Update: Local squirrels are pleased to announce Carl W. Mishler of New Market, Virginia, passed away on November 23, 2020.

Three years of Carl was pretty much all we could take and we listed our property for sale. A gay couple bought it which I'm sure Carl would have been pleased about. Holly and I placed an offer on a craftsman style home, a lot closer to restaurants, and it was accepted. The home was built in 1911 but was renovated in 2011. The former owner, an elderly widow, left the house to her eight cats when she died in 2007, with instructions and money for them to be fed. There were over two-hundred cats when they cleared the place out in 2010. Three years of cat urine does a lot of damage to wood and everything had to gutted. Walls, stairs and floors were torn out. The house probably lost a lot of its character in the process but aspects still exist; it has tall ceilings and large windows and no wardrobe space. Apparently the house is well known locally and whenever we tell people where we moved to, we're met with, "Oh, you bought the cat house." Holly liked the name and had a brass plate made with *The Cat House* engraved on it. It was on the wall by the front door for a while but then someone told her 'cat house' is another name for a brothel so she took it down.

Our new home didn't have a fence so it was the first thing I added when we moved here. I didn't build it myself, I paid someone else to do it, but only because I don't own a tractor with a backhoe attachment to dig post-holes with. I wanted a twenty-foot fence, because I shouldn't have to look at our neighbour's shitty yard from our nice yard, but I was told six-feet is the maximum height allowed by law because police officers have to be able to climb over it.

Firstly, I don't want police officers climbing over my fence. Secondly, the police officers in our town would be lucky to make it over a knee-high fence. If they're meant to be able to climb over six-foot fences, why are 4XL uniforms a thing? It's just enabling. Are they tested on their ability to climb fences in cadet training or is it just a vague goal?

"Okay cadets, today's test is to see if you can climb over a six-foot fence. Dennis, you're up."
"Are we allowed to use a ladder?"
"Do you have a ladder, Dennis?"
"Yes."
"Well that's fine then. Greg, hold the ladder for Dennis."

Our fence is made out of some kind of plastic so I doubt it would support the weight anyway. Plus we have a gate.

"Couldn't we just go through the gate?"
"Sorry, Greg?"
"There's a gate. We could just go through that. It would save mucking about with the ladder."
"Right, I hope everyone else is paying attention because Greg just suggested using the gate. Well done, Greg, police officering isn't just about climbing fences and discounts at Burger King, it's also about improvisation."

The second thing I did to our house was install exterior security cameras. If police officers are climbing over our fence, I want enough warning to erase my Internet history.

The third thing I did to the house, a deck extension, took a bit longer and cost more than the first two things. I calculated the project would take two weeks and cost one thousand dollars to finish, and I wasn't too far off at six months and just under twelve grand.

I blame the budget blowout entirely on Trump's tariffs on wood from Canadian mills driving up lumber prices. And on forgetting to include the cost of nails, screws, cement, cinder blocks, rebar, paint, rollers, and tools. The time blowout can be partly attributed to the fact that the original plans kept changing, and partly due to my construction experience consisting entirely of watching time-lapse videos on YouTube.

"You're adding a koi pond?"
"Yes, incorporated into the deck."
"How much extra time will that add to the construction?"
"Eight minutes and sixteen seconds."

I use the word 'plans' loosely in the paragraph above. There were no blueprints that some professional architect spent months tweaking. No project manager on site unrolling said blueprints and giving a little nod then pointing at things. The plans were drawn on the back of Comcast bill with a Sharpie, and included measurements such as 'twelve and a half big steps' and 'four metal frogs and a didit'. The actual length of a 'didit' was never defined but became a standard throughout the project.

"How long does this piece of wood need to be, Seb?"
"Three crusty work gloves and a didit."
"Long didit or short didit?"
"Standard didit."

Using inches wasn't an option because neither Seb or I could work out how to read the measuring tape.

"It's... four feet, six and three-quarter inches, and a tenth and one sixth of a barleycorn."
"What?"
"I'll just make a mark on the measuring tape with a Sharpie."

The deck probably would have taken double the time to build if Seb wasn't here to help me. He flew from Australia to the United States in December of 2019, for his yearly three-month visit, but then couldn't fly back due to the pandemic. I was selfishly happy when Seb couldn't leave; the hardest thing I've had to do every year, for the last ten years, is drive him to the airport and say goodbye. It meant he overstayed his tourist Visa, so was technically an illegal alien, but ICE doesn't give a fuck unless you look Mexican. Nobody is separating Swedish families and locking their blonde haired, blue eyed kids up in cages.

"Snälla, jag vill bara ha min mamma och pappa."
"Shut it, Birkenstock, be thankful for your Utåker bed and Tjärblomster blanket."
"Min filt kliar och jag är olycklig."

Around April, Seb decided he wanted to stay in the United States and make it his home. His biological mother wasn't happy about the decision but, as Seb is over the age of eighteen, her permission wasn't needed or sought. It works out better for her anyway; she can now entertain clients at her house instead of a mattress under a bridge.

Seb gave several reasons for his decision, but I suspect it boiled down to faster Internet and a girl named Rebekah he met at a New Year's Eve party. They started dating and were inseparable until the pandemic gave me a viable excuse to ban her from our house. I don't dislike Rebekah but not disliking someone isn't the same as wanting them around. She's whiny and annoying and when she isn't treated like royalty, she sulks. Everyone's entitled to a bit of a sulk every now and then, life's unfair and shit happens, but Rebekah's sulking is constant and unrelenting. It's not the adult version of sulking either, the one where you act a bit sullen and make yourself a coffee without asking if anyone else wants one, it's the toddler version of sulking where you stick out your bottom lip and make a face like you're pushing out a particularly difficult poo. Except practiced for eighteen years until it's an art form. Sometimes Rebekah's 'lip-jut poo-push face' is the result of understandable annoyances, such as having to ride a unicorn floaty when she wanted the duck, but I've also witnessed it while she was paddling a kayak, singing karaoke, and riding an ATV. Who sulks while riding an ATV? It's impossible not to have a good time on an ATV.

Cute girls get a 'princess pass' because it's acceptable to act entitled when you're good looking. It's a rule or something. Life is easier when you're attractive so the moments when life isn't easy are more traumatizing. Rebekah isn't attractive though, so she doesn't get a pass for anything.

"What's the issue, Rebekah?"
"Nothing."
"What's with the face then?"
"What face?"
"The lip-jut poo-push face."
"What?"
"That's what I call it. It's dreadful. Cover your head with a towel or something so I don't have to look at it."

Rebekah's bewilderment at not being the center of everyone's universe may be unwarranted, but it is understandable; I've seen her mother's Facebook posts. Kim, Rebekah's mother, is Rebekah's best friend, director of marketing, official photographer, and president of the Rebekah Fan Club. She's like a 'dance mom' without the talented child. Kim's latest post is a photo of Rebekah at a supermarket, sticking her arse out while pushing a shopping cart, with the caption, "Who's the cutest girl in Food Lion?" Earlier posts are essentially the same but in different locations; Rebekah isn't just the cutest girl in a supermarket, she's also the cutest girl in a quilt museum, a Chinese buffet, a laundromat, a Dollar General store, a beach in winter, a movie theatre, and a dentist's waiting room.

If you scroll far enough down Kim's Facebook page, you get to the photos of Rebekah before she lost weight.

"Who's the cutest girl in Starbucks?"
"I've no idea, Kim, I wasn't there. Ask the heifer if she knows."

I'm allowed to make fat jokes because I currently have a bit of a tummy. It's like gay guys being allowed to use the word faggot or black people being allowed to ask other black people where they got their bike from. As an honorary jolly person, I understand all too well how hard it is to lose a few cats; I did four sit ups last week and didn't notice any difference so I've no idea how Rebekah managed to shrink to a tenth of her original size. I have heard that it takes twenty-eight muscles to smile and forty-two to frown, so it's possible Rebekah's lip-jut poo-push face uses every muscle available and burns a lot of calories in the process.

Praise and encouragement are integral parts of parenting, but there needs to be balance; if you're taught that you're special, better, a ten when you're really a four, an inflated notion of importance is to be expected. It's why I randomly tell Seb he's 'not all that.'

Nobody is all that. Except Anne Hathaway obviously. Seb is okay for the most part though; he's caring and kind and a solid seven in the looks department, maybe an eight on a good hair day. Seb is also extremely easy-going; nothing much gets to him and he rarely complains. I think the last time he sulked was ten years ago when I sprayed him with a pressure washer and almost tore off his left nipple.

Seb's 'everything's fine' approach to life and Rebekah's perpetual dismay at the unfairness of it isn't a tale of opposites attracting or love being blind, it's more like one of those news stories where two people with Down syndrome get married and show you around their apartment.

"And this is our kettle. Auntie Ruth gave us that."

Early in their relationship, I asked Seb how he coped with Rebekah's sulking, and he stated, "It doesn't bother me."

"You can't be serious. You're an enabler."
"Please. She's not an alcoholic or drug addict."
"No, she's worse. She's a pouter. And you're a pout permitter. You and Kim should get matching *Team Rebekah* t-shirts. Or maybe jackets. Rebekah used to be fat, did you know?"
"So?"
"I just don't want you to be surprised when you eventually see her naked and her skin is flappy. That's what happens when people lose a lot of weight. Their skin gets flappy and makes slapping noises when they run. I saw it on *The Biggest Loser*."
"Fat shaming is a form of bullying. Be best."
"I apologise. My comments were uncalled for and I will endeavour to be less judgmental. Will you be my friend?"
"Yes."

Update: I didn't have to do much endeavouring because Seb broke up with Rebekah last week. I asked him if it was because of her flappy skin and he said that her skin wasn't flappy, he'd just realised that while being separated during the pandemic, he didn't miss her as much as he thought he would. "Plus," he added, "I'm not sure if you ever noticed, but she sulks a lot."

Having Seb permanently move to America meant making a few sacrifices - he eats a lot and his bathroom smells like a hamster cage - but Holly and I both hate doing housework and having him around is like having an indentured servant. We filled out a lot of residency paperwork and wrote a lot of cheques. I also Photoshopped a fake letter from Homeland Security, with Seb's immigration number and details listed, stating that his permanent residency application had been denied and, as his Visa was expired, he had twenty-four hours to leave the country or face deportation. I folded the letter and placed it inside a Homeland Security envelope that we'd previously received, then pretended to open and read the letter to myself while mumbling, 'Oh no, this is terrible," and, "What are we are going to do?" while Seb was in the room. If someone had recorded the scene, I'd probably be looking at an Academy award. I handed the letter to Seb to read and his reaction was a lot better than I'd anticipated. I thought he'd be upset and possibly panic, but he just looked sad and nodded and took the dog for a walk. I could tell he'd been crying when he got back, so I felt bad and told him it was a joke. Not right away though, the next day while he was packing.

And yes, I realize Birkenstock is a German brand, not Swedish. I originally wrote Hasselblad a few pages back, which *is* a Swedish brand, but Seb asked if Hasselblad is Swedish for someone with a bladder problem so I changed it. I could have used IKEA of course, but then I would have had to change the bed and blanket name bit and I don't know enough about Sweden to come up with another joke. I do know Volvos, ABBA, and Greta Thunberg come from Sweden, and that all Swedish women, apart from Greta Thunberg, play volleyball, but that's about the extent of my knowledge. I'm making an assumption of course; Greta may play volleyball when she's not too busy waving at penguins or whatever it is she does. And, just so I don't receive dozens of emails telling me off for belittling the important work Greta is doing, I'm fully aware that climate change is a very real threat and that it is our collective and individual responsibility to preserve the planet on which we all live. I just think she'd be a lot prettier if she smiled more.

I actually dated an environmental activist once. At least I thought we were dating. Her name was Yolanda, which is apparently Polish for 'the unwashed'. We spent 48 hours chained to a tree on a housing development, then she informed me she was a lesbian and had just needed a ride. It's not easy getting a refund for Greenpeace membership. I had to ring my bank and dispute the credit card charge. I did get to keep the T-shirt though. Really, I deserved it for everything I'd done for the environment. There was a lot of sap on that tree.

I also owned a Hasselblad once. For those not familiar with the brand, Hasselblad makes nice medium format cameras. I got mine at an auction of dead people's stuff that my friend Bill dragged me to. It was my first estate auction but Bill attended them regularly - I'm not sure why, I guess when you reach a certain age you just start looking for things to do with yourself on weekends.

"Anything planned for this weekend, Gerald?"
"Yes, lots. I'm going to walk aimlessly around a mall, buy a Consumer Cellular flip-phone, pay for groceries with a cheque, and check out the bonus *Jeopardy!* questions on J!6."

As the owner of Australia's leading caravan and camping guide, Bill could easily afford new stuff, but he liked dead people's stuff more. Especially their suitcases. Bill once bid for, and won, a complete set of Louis Vuitton travel luggage for seven hundred dollars. It was a pretty good score in and of itself, but, after taking the luggage home and inspecting each suitcase, he discovered, inside a toiletry bag, an envelope containing a passport and twelve thousand dollars. It wasn't a huge amount of money to Bill - he once flew to England to buy shoes - but the amount wasn't important, it was the fact that the 'fat bitch' who had bid against him didn't get the money. It became an obsession after that. Bill was convinced that every dead person has an envelope of cash hidden in one of their belongings, and that he was gifted with some kind of Sherlock Holmes level deduction ability that enabled him to guess which belonging it was.

"And next up we have a walnut chest of drawers. I'll start the bidding at three hundred dollars..."

"What do you think, Bill? Four or five envelopes stuffed with cash in that?'

"No, too obvious. You'd have to be an idiot to hide your cash in a chest of drawers. I'm going to bid on the cuckoo clock, the cello, and the box of assorted hats."

I'm not sure if it was because Bill bid for and won so many auction items, or if he did actually have some kind of deductive ability, but he was right a surprising amount of the time. Most of his discovered riches over the years were in the one to five hundred dollar range, but he did score twelve hundred dollars in old wooden shoe-shine box, two grand inside a fishing tackle box, fifteen hundred dollars in an electric kettle, and a Rolex watch in an old Kodak camera bag - which was one of several items in a 'box of assorted photography equipment' that Bill paid four hundred dollars for. Other items in the box included lenses, a tripod, half a dozen Canon, Nikon, Pentax and Leica cameras... and a Hasselblad 503CW - complete with winder, lens and user manual.

"Oh my god, it's a Hasselblad."

"Is it digital?"

"No, but it's still a nice camera. You could sell it."

"Yes, I'll pop down to the local pawn shop first thing tomorrow morning and see if they'll give me enough for my next heroin fix."

Bill gave me the Hasselblad. His phone had a camera and he didn't have any use for "antiquated shit that takes film." I didn't have any use for the camera either, but I thought it was cool so I displayed it on a bookshelf at home, next to a rock that may have been a meteorite and a scale model of the rocket from *Tintin on the Moon*. It served as a book end and dust collector for several years until a photographer I knew offered to buy it for three hundred dollars, and I looked online to see if that was a reasonable price.

"Two thousand dollars and it's yours."

"That's outrageous."

"No, that's half what it's worth. Offering me three hundred was outrageous. I'm actually kind of pissed you tried to take advantage of my ignorance."

"Fine. I'll give you a thousand dollars for it."

"Two thousand, three hundred."

"You can't go up. That's not how this works."

"Two thousand, seven hundred."

"Fine, I'll give you two thousand dollars."

"Sorry, it's not for sale."

I was glad I didn't sell it because when Bill died, it was the only possession I had to remind me of him. He was only seventy and in good health when a texting driver veered onto the wrong side of the road and hit Bill's parked car while he was loading a pair of floor speakers into the trunk. Bill died instantly, which is what everyone likes to hear, the texting driver lost her four-year-old daughter and her legs.

I've never understood why people text while driving. It's like playing the game Operation while riding a horse. Except the horse is made out of metal and glass and going seventy miles per hour and other metal and glass horses are all around you and headed the other direction with only a few feet between. You're eight times *it's hard to* more likely to be in *concentrate on* an accident *two things* if you're texting on *at the same time* a mobile phone. Holly texts me while she's driving all the time and, when I berate her about it, she declares, "I'm capable of doing more than one thing at a time." Which is true of most people but it's hardly going to stand up as a viable justification in court if you're responsible for an accident.

"If I understand this correctly, Mrs Thorne, you were playing Twister, reading a book, and changing your pants when you drove through a school crossing and killed fifteen children. Do you have anything to say in your defence?"
"I'm capable of doing more than one thing at a time."
"Yes, most people are. Excellent point. Case dismissed."

I won't even answer calls when I'm driving let alone read and reply to text messages.

"I rang you thirty times and you didn't answer. What if I was abducted and locked in the trunk of someone's car?"
"Were you abducted, Holly?"
"No, but I can't find the Scotch tape and I need to attach a feather to the end of a pen. Did you put it somewhere?"

When I was told that Bill died instantly, my first thought was that nobody dies instantly in an accident unless they're vaporised. There has to be a moment where they think 'what the fuck' or 'dear god that hurts' before their brain neurons stop firing. I read somewhere that during the French Revolution, when thousands of heads were being lopped off to thunderous applause, the decapitated heads often blinked and opened and closed their mouths as if trying to speak. "They died instantly" is just a kind lie to help the dead person's family and friends feel better about the whole thing.

"If it's any consolation, he died instantly. His lower half was crushed between two parked cars and he convulsed and flailed for approximately two minutes until the brain neurons ceased firing."
"How is that instant?"
"The bit where he died was instant."
"What about the convulsing and flailing bit?"
"That doesn't count. The trick is in the wording; he *died* instantly. Everyone does."

Bill's sister Elizabeth flew from England to arrange the service and finalize his estate. He had no other family so it was nice of her to bother. There were around fifteen people at the service, most of them from the caravaning and camping industry. I said a few words about Bill's love of action movies, his addiction to auctions, and his refusal to leave the house if it was windy because he knew someone who was killed by a tree branch.

I offered to meet Elizabeth at Bill's house the next day, but she told me she'd hired a company to handle his estate and belongings. I went anyway and let myself in with the key Bill hid under a fake rock by the front door. It was weird walking around his house without him there - quiet and still. Whenever I'd visited the house previously, there was always a television or music playing in the background. I guess to keep Bill company. I made my way into the living room and turned on the television.

On the wall to the right of the television, there was a framed print of a bluebird by the American artist Charley Harper. It was a signed limited edition and was the only item I remember Bill bidding for at an auction because he liked it, not because it might contain hidden treasure. There'd been a bit of a bidding war for it, between Bill and a fat lady, and when Bill won, the lady glared at him and he gave her the finger. We'd stopped at a hardware store on the drive home so he could buy a hook to hang it with, and I'd held the frame to the wall while Bill stood back and instructed, "A little higher, a little to your left."

Through the kitchen window, I could see the yellow bird feeder that Bill always kept full. It was empty so I let myself out the sliding back door and refilled it from the box of birdseed Bill kept in the cupboard above the toaster. Then, figuring the feeder wouldn't be filled again, I emptied the rest of the box onto the window sill to give the birds a final banquet.

I unplugged the kitchen appliances and turned off the taps leading to the washing machine. Every time I went away for business or on vacation, Bill told me to turn my washing machine taps off in case a hose splits and floods the apartment. I never remembered to do it but I always told him I had.

A white monogrammed bathrobe had fallen off the hook in the upstairs bathroom, I hung it back up. I'd never been in Bill's bedroom but it was exactly how I expected it would be. The bed was made and clothes were put away. I gave the room a quick search for anything Bill wouldn't want anyone else discovering, like porn or massive dildos, but there wasn't anything like that.

Making my way back downstairs, I turned off the lights and television, locked the front door behind me, and hid the key under the fake rock.

The law firm handling Bill's estate rang me a week or so later and asked me to come in. I admit I entertained thoughts of Bill having bequeathed me his house or a ton of money in his will, or maybe something odd like a telescope that you couldn't look through because it was blocked by a hidden envelope full of cash inside, but I was just asked to sign for a metal urn containing Bill's ashes. Apparently Elizabeth had flown back to England and just left them. I did look inside the urn when I got home, to check if there was an envelope, but that would have been a pretty difficult trick to set up.

I've never been bequeathed anything in a will. I've seen television shows and movies where family members dressed in black are sitting in a lawyer's office listening in anticipation as a will is read, but they're generally families that have money. Someone gets bequeathed a house and a million dollars and someone scowls and says they'll fight it in court. A will reading for anyone in our family would sound like someone who works at Goodwill listing off the contents of a box left at the back door.

"And to David, I bequeath my four-slice toaster, eight teaspoons, and a fitted sheet."

I know a woman named Heather King who recently scored 100K in life insurance after her husband Ian died. His death was unexpected and she has a new boyfriend already. This isn't a joke; I just want it on record that I think it's a bit suss.

The closest I've ever come to inheriting something is when my father died and I found a George Foreman grill and two large boxes of pornography in his shed. It wasn't even good pornography, mostly Playboy and VHS cassettes with titles like *New Wave Hookers* and *Massage Parlour Wives*. I didn't even bother watching them, which says a lot as I once masturbated to an episode of *20/20*. At the bottom of one of the boxes, there was an envelope and an inflatable sex doll. The envelope contained Polaroid Instamatic photos, which I burned, and the sex doll was brittle and cracked where it had been folded. The vagina bit still worked though.

135

When my mother died last year, my sister Leith kept it a secret. My mother and I weren't close and Leith probably didn't want to share the proceeds from the sale of her estate. It didn't bother me; she needs the money more than I do. It can't be easy raising five kids from five different fathers who are all either in prison or gave false names and addresses and can't be located.

"Who's my dad?"
"Lamp Couch Hallway. He had brown hair just like yours."
"Will I ever meet him?"
"No, he's an astronaut and lives on the moon. Hush now, finish your 1/5th of the Big Mac then get ready for bed. It's your turn to have the blanket tonight."
"Yay!"

I once lent Leith five hundred dollars, to fix the transmission on her van, and she bought an above ground pool instead. I never saw a cent of the money again and I never went for a swim because it was an above ground pool. Even if you build a deck around an above ground pool, everyone knows what it is. Nobody says, "Oh really? It's an above ground pool? You'd never be able to tell." They say, "Oh, the invite didn't mention it's an above ground pool. I wouldn't have come if I'd known." Maybe not to your face but that's what they're saying. Leith didn't have a deck around her pool so everyone just sat in Coleman camping chairs looking up at it. I mentioned the money a few years later and Leith stated, "I bought you a pool float."

The truth is, Bill and I weren't close enough for him to mention me in a will. We'd been friends for over a decade and enjoyed each other's company, but our relationship consisted almost entirely of attending auctions and sometimes having a drink and meal afterwards. We didn't share any mutual friends or even mutual interests really. Apart from auctions and action movies, I don't even remember what we talked about over meals; maybe what we'd watched on television during the week and the latest work gossip?

When I sat at my laptop to write something meaningful to say at Bill's service, something that would make everyone in the audience nod and smile knowingly, I stared at a blank page for thirty minutes, Googled 'nice things to say at someone's funeral', and copied and pasted someone else's text. I added some stuff about tree branches and a joke about Bill being contacted by the television show *Hoarders* regarding all the suitcases in his garage, but I forgot to change the name in one sentence and a few people frowned and looked at me oddly when I mentioned Pat's love of Bruce Willis movies.

"Who's Pat?"
"Sorry?"
"You said Pat loved Bruce Willis movies."
"Oh, Pat was just my nickname for Bill. It's short for Patypuss Bill. As in 'platypus bill' but with patypuss instead of platypuss. Because Bill liked patting cats."

I'm not overly proficient at coming up with believable lies on the spot. I understand the key is to keep the lie simple, so it's easier to remember and can be expanded upon if pressed, but for some reason I always panic and convolute the lie with details to prove it isn't a lie. I once told a client his artwork was late because I was in a Bangladesh kite-fighting accident. I wore a bandage on my hand to our next meeting and said something about my cousin marrying a man from Bangladesh, named Hububu, who she met overseas while researching unitary parliamentary democracies and constitutional republics. There may have also been some stuff about snakes and textile exports. I also once told a lady in an elevator, after she asked where I bought my scarf, that I'd knitted it myself - because I didn't want to admit that it was from Target - and that the wool I used was hand-spun from my pet alpaca.

My Uncle Carl used to say, "If you always tell the truth, you won't need to remember all the lies you've ever told." While sound in theory, after he was hit and killed by a train while attempting to jump across platforms, my mother went through his belongings and discovered a collection of love letters, spanning two decades, between Carl and a man named Donald. My mother had no idea her own brother was gay so he must have been lying his entire life. With hindsight, I should have known. I stayed overnight at his house once, while my parents were at the hospital with my sister, and he convinced me to have a bath with him by telling me that it was a Japanese custom.

He wasn't Japanese so I have no idea why I agreed to it, but we'd both been drinking saké beforehand which may have had something to with it. I was eight. Nobody got hurt though and we both got something out of it. Carl got to see me naked and I got a scarf when we went shopping the next day.

"It looks fantastic on you. Very Bohemian."

I wore the scarf for almost a year, regardless of the temperature. I had no idea what Bohemian meant but I knew it had something to do with the band Queen and the movie *Flash Gordon* was very popular at the time.

My parents were at the hospital because my older sister Leith had swallowed twelve dollars in five-cent pieces and was being kept overnight for observation. It was the third time she had been admitted for swallowing coins. Nobody knew why she kept doing it. I asked her about it years later, and she said that she just liked the taste. Apparently she sucked the coins until they had no flavour left and then swallowed them so they didn't get mixed up with the unsucked coins.

Bill didn't like patting cats. He hated them. I wish I'd included that fact in my speech as it would have forced me to come up with something better than 'patypuss'. Fifteen years later, I'll be lying in bed, about to fall asleep, and think, "Really David? Patypuss?"

I knew a lot more things that Bill hated than things he liked. Perhaps that's the reason I can't remember what we talked about - because our only discourse was complaining. I know he hated cats, loud dishwashers, wet bath mats, kids, wind, the beach, and probably being crushed. I should have asked him more about things he liked, gotten to know who he was rather than what he did. I wish I'd at least asked him what he'd like done with his ashes.

I had no idea what I was supposed to do with them. Was I meant to keep them and, if asked what was in the metal urn, answer, "That's an old guy I used to go to auctions with"? Was I meant to scatter them somewhere? Bill hated everywhere. I do remember him once saying he'd like to visit Bali one day, but our friendship wasn't worth a five-hour flight. I hate flying.

The ashes sat on my bookshelf next to the Hasselblad for a few months until Seb rinsed out the urn to use as a playhouse for Mr Steve, his hamster, while I was in the shower.

Not all the ashes had been rinsed down the sink, there was a mushy pile, about a teaspoon worth, surrounding the lip of the drain. I wiped it up with a sponge and put the sponge in a sandwich bag for safekeeping. The next day at work, I put the sandwich bag in a padded envelope, stuck ten dollars worth of stamps on it, and mailed it, without a return address, to the Nandini Resort and Spa in Bali, Indonesia.

I'm not sure what happened to the urn or if it matters. After Mr Steve was sucked into a vacuum cleaner hose, then shot out when the airflow was reversed, his cage was put in the garage and eventually thrown out when Holly and I packed to move to the United States. We threw out a lot of stuff at the time. It's hard enough deciding what to pack in a suitcase when you're going on vacation let alone moving to live in a different country. I sacrificed most of my clothes in favour of stuff that had sentimental value; my collection of first edition John Wyndham novels, a ceramic rooster I stole from a friend's kitchen, and the Hasselblad that Bill gave me. I trashed fridge magnets and other kipple, dropped off thirty or so boxes of clothes and household goods at Goodwill, and listed our furniture and car online. We needed the money; it's not cheap to start again from scratch.

It was actually the second time I'd experienced starting from scratch. The third if you count leaving home when I was fourteen. When I was ten, my sister Leith draped her dressing gown over a chair in front of a bar heater and it caught fire. This was before clothing had fire safety ratings and her dressing gown was probably made out of lint and wax. My family was watching *The Love Boat* at the time and my mother asked, "What's that smell?" seconds before the dressing gown went 'whoomph'. Everyone yelled and carried on like pork chops and my father kicked over the chair the dressing gown was on. Grabbing a sofa pillow, he beat at the flames, which only seemed to fan them higher, and then the pillow caught fire. I can't recall what the rest of us were doing, but nobody followed the *Get down low and go, go, go!* fire safety rule. As my father thrashed at the flames with the fire-pillow, fireballs of stuffing flew everywhere and the curtains went up. Reevaluating the situation, my father cast aside the fire-pillow and ran outside to get the garden hose. Earlier that day, my friend Michael and I were playing in the backyard and had decided to make a flying fox. We didn't have a pulley to use but devised one out of a golf cart wheel and a bicycle handle that worked fairly well. We didn't have any rope either.

My father blamed the house burning down on the garden hose being stretched and tied between two trees. Which is hardly fair. Sure, maybe Michael and I should have untied the hose and put it back after we realized it was too stretchy, but if Leith had been more careful with her dressing gown or my father hadn't spread the fire, the lack of a water delivery system wouldn't have been an issue. For years afterwards, whenever someone lit birthday candles or did anything with matches, my father would declare, "Hang on, I'd better check David hasn't used the hose to make a flying fox before you light that," then he'd laugh as if it was the wittiest joke ever told. Firstly, it wasn't, and secondly, why would I use the hose as a flying fox line a second time when it hadn't worked the first time? Yes, I felt partly responsible for the loss of our possessions, but reminding everyone of it constantly didn't achieve anything apart from making me wish he'd been trapped in the fire when he ran back inside to save his new tennis racquet.

Our house didn't completely burn to the ground, it was made out of bricks, but a section of the roof caved in and possessions that weren't burnt or melted, were damaged by smoke, soot, and water from the firetrucks. A few unmeltable knickknacks were recovered later but almost everything else was gone. It was as if one minute we had a home, with my own bedroom and posters and *Star Wars* figurines, then suddenly we were homeless, like refugees or a family of hobos, with nothing but the clothes we were wearing and my father's Slazenger.

"Is that what you ran back in for? Your tennis racquet?"
"It's signed by John McEnroe."
"No, it isn't. That's just a sticker. He didn't personally sign it himself. Why didn't you save our wedding album and family photos?"
"Well let's not worry about that now. They're just possessions. The important thing is that everyone is okay."
"Everyone and your tennis racquet."
"I have a semi-final match next week."

The tennis racquet had been a present. From my father to himself. He'd also bought my mother a tennis racquet but it wasn't a John McEnroe edition Slazenger, it was a shitty Wilson. I'm fairly certain he only bought the Wilson so he could say, "I bought *us* tennis racquets." For Christmas one year, my father bought my mother a lambswool steering wheel cover for her car. It was the wrong size so he put it on his steering wheel. The year before that, he gave her a set of plastic picnic tumblers with his favourite football team's logo on them, and a year's subscription to Sports Illustrated. For her birthday one year, he blindfolded and led her outside to reveal a ride-on lawnmower he'd bought himself. We only had a quarter-acre block and most of the yard was concrete because my parents bought the house from a Greek family. The first thing they did when we moved in was remove a twelve-foot concrete fountain shaped like a rearing horse from the front yard. They had to bring in a crane. The ride-on mower cut my father's gardening time down dramatically though, it took less than a minute to complete the small patch of lawn in the backyard and that included driving the mower out of the shed and putting it back. He let me have a go on it once but I ran over a concrete gnome and wasn't allowed near it after that. I also went a year without pocket-money to pay for new blades.

We stayed at my grandparent's house for about a week until my father and grandfather had a fight over how thinly onions should be sliced. My grandfather and my father had never got along. They once had a swordfight with a rake and a weed-whacker after my father parked on my grandfather's lawn, and my father had to be taken to the hospital for stitches. We moved into a furnished apartment for three months while our house was being rebuilt. With our temporary accommodation and new clothes to replace the ones we'd lost, it was like being in a witness protection program. I told the next door neighbour my name was Alex Knight and I owned a pet shark.

Right up until the moment we walked back into our house, I'd assumed it would be identical to how it was before the fire - that the builders would put back the same floor coverings, the same furniture, the same laundry door frame with head heights marked in Sharpie, and the same misaligned section of bamboo-patterned wallpaper behind the television. It wasn't though. It was all different. All new. The walls, previously yellowed by years of cigarette smoke, were freshly painted in pastels. The carpet, once worn Kermit green was now pebble-beige Berber. Our velour couch and vinyl bean bags were replaced with a modular lounge, and our Rank Arena fourteen-inch television set had been replaced with a massive twenty-one-inch Sanyo. As we walked through our new home, wearing our new clothes and new shoes, we were like a better version of us. A new us.

"These are nice pants. You don't want to pack these pants?"

"No, Holly. I can buy new pants in America."

"Why would you leave perfectly good pants behind?"

"I don't need them. Besides, I don't have room in my suitcase to pack anything else."

"It's not *what* you pack, it's *how* you pack. The trick is to put things inside of things. Like shirts inside of shoes. Have you put things inside of things?"

"Honestly, I don't need any of it. I'll start from scratch. New country, new me."

"We don't have the money for that. Give me a look... Right, you can fit two pairs of socks in this ceramic rooster and... how do you open this big camera?"

145

We bought a Jeep Grand Cherokee with the six thousand dollars that was hidden inside the Hasselblad. It was second hand but clean and only had forty thousand miles on it. There was even enough left over for new pants and some to go towards Holly's engagement ring. It probably wouldn't have been enough to have 'Will you marry me?" written in fireworks, but the money helped a lot during our first few months in the United States - I wasn't working then and we were still waiting on my first royalty cheque from Penguin. Later, I sold the Hasselblad on eBay to pay for our honeymoon in Mexico. I didn't need it to remember Bill, I had the pants.

Also, on my father's fifty-eighth birthday, a few months before he died of prostate cancer, Seb and I visited his house in Thebarton. It had been several months since we'd last visited, since there'd been any reason to visit. All he ever did was watch the football or cricket on television and I've never been interested in either. We ate pizza and watched the test match between Australia and England. After the meal, I brought out a birthday cake that Seb and I had purchased from a supermarket on the way. It had a picture of a girl playing hockey on it but it had been the only one left on the shelf. I'd also purchased two candles, in the shape of a five and an eight. I placed the candles on the cake and handed Seb a cigarette lighter to light them with.

"Hang on," my father said, "I'd better check David hasn't used the hose to make a flying fox before you light that."

To: All Staff
From: Jennifer Haines
Date: Monday 6 April 2020 10.12am
Subject: Zoom meetings

Good morning,

I drove past the office this morning and it was quite sad seeing the blinds closed. On a positive note, I think our first Zoom production meeting went well. There are still a few bugs to be ironed out but Gary is going to check his settings before the next meeting and David has promised not to use an airhorn when Ben is speaking. If everyone treats others with the same courtesy as they do in the office, the next meeting will be more productive.

Mike wants a paragraph added to the website explaining that office meetings are by appointment only and that we're not closed, just working remotely. Ben, can you have a look at wording this and get something to David in the next day or so? We should probably also add it to our email signatures.

Walter, I've asked you to use the standard email signature format several times now. You cannot advertise personal items for sale on company emails.

David, I received your timesheets but when I opened the file it was just a recipe for cauliflower and broccoli cheese crepes. Please check and resend.

Thank you, Jen

My metabolism must have slowed over the years because it wasn't difficult to gain weight during the pandemic. It would have been nice if all the cauliflower and broccoli cheese crêpes I've eaten filled me out evenly, but it's as if everything I swallow enters my stomach and says, "Here's good."

The only thing worse than looking like a stick insect is looking like a pregnant stick insect. Actually, that's a bit of an overstatement, I'm sure there are plenty of things worse than looking like a pregnant stick insect. Being raped for instance. Or being captured by ISIS and having your head cut off. Or having actor Josh Gad's head. It wouldn't matter what type of physique you had if you had Josh Gad's head. If I had Josh Gad's head and was captured by ISIS, I'd be happy for them to cut it off.

"Again with the Josh Gad comments David? Your Twitter argument with him was six years ago. You have to let it go."
"Never!"

I had to go up a waist size in pants which makes the legs all flappy. Nobody likes flappy pant legs. It was to be expected I suppose; working from home has meant easy access to the refrigerator and less low-level activity throughout the day. Even with a desk job I still had to walk to my car to get to work, walk throughout the day, walk to lunch, and find new hiding spots. It's not exactly high-intensity training but at least there was some movement. Last week I spent a whole day in a hammock eating Goldfish crackers.

"Your camera is off, David. I did mention in the email that this was going to be a video meeting."

"Yes, Mike, but I remember what everyone looks like so it seemed a bit pointless."

"It's not about how people look, it's about communication. Expressions of satisfaction, concern, or understanding can't be effectively communicated without video... what's that crunching noise?"

The only expression of satisfaction I witnessed during our last video meeting was when Walter, our junior designer, picked his nose for several minutes and finally scooped out what appeared to be a two-inch alien slug.

"That was probably the third most disgusting thing I have ever seen, Walter."

"What?"

"That huge booger."

"What booger?"

"The booger you just excavated from your left nostril. It was the size of a pickle."

'I wasn't picking my nose, I was scratching it."

"No you weren't. I took a screenshot. Where did you wipe it? It looked like it was on your pants."

"You can't see my pants."

Other highlights included Ben, our copywriter, wearing a jacket and tie in front of a background of Shanghai at night like he was a guest on CNN, and Gary, our account manager, using a potato as a webcam; his video stream was made up of about sixteen pixels and looked like a flickering Rubik's Cube. The audio lag was also so bad it was like communicating with someone in space.

"And that's why..."

"..."

'And that's why what, Gary?'

"..."

"Okay, Gary seems to be hav..."

"we can't quote for client work that is additional..."

"Sure, but th..."

"to the original quote... sorry, did you say something..."

"No, I thou..."

"while I was talking, Mike? I missed..."

"No, go on."

";it."

"Okay, does anyone else have anything to discu..."

"Over."

We've only had three video meetings since the pandemic began. They were originally intended to be weekly but the first was just an hour of everyone fiddling with their settings and commenting on everyone else's bedroom, living room, kitchen, or city skyline, and the second was cancelled ten minutes in after Melissa, our secretary, told Jodie, our senior designer, that her head looks big on camera, and Jodie informed Melissa that at least she wasn't a skank ho cumslut with fucked up teeth.

To: All Staff
From: Jennifer Haines
Date: Friday 10 April 2020 12.47pm
Subject: Respect

Happy Easter everyone,

As most of you are aware, this morning's Zoom meeting didn't go well and there are a couple of areas I think we can all work on to improve the experience for everyone:

1. Words have weight. Please be mindful of others feelings and treat others as you expect to be treated. This includes shouting over people, making derogatory comments, and saying "Okay boomer."

2. Courtesy is contagious. Negative comments about the furniture in someone's house is disrespectful. David, nobody asked for your opinion about floral curtains. Personally, I find your mid-century modern decor cold and depressing.

3. Be prepared. It's not just a Scout motto. If a meeting is scheduled for 11am, please shower before the meeting starts, not while it's underway. I'm not pointing the finger at you Walter, this applies to everyone.

Mike, I spoke to Jodie and Melissa. Melissa has accepted Jodie's apology. I'm updating the employee workplace agreement to include video conferencing behavior and will email everyone a copy early next week.

Thank you, Jen

Jodie and Melissa were almost fired last year due to their 'inability to conduct themselves in a professional manner'. They were actually informed their services were no longer required and their E-92 employment termination forms were completed, but then they both turned up at the office and had a meeting with Mike and Jennifer during which Jodie and Melissa cried and said that they were best friends now and were sorry for breaking an expensive Arco floor lamp and would pay for it and would never fight again.

There was an office pool to guess how long Jodie and Melissa could keep up the 'best friends' facade. Walter was the closest with his bet of four days. He was stoked about winning until he was told he had to buy rounds at the pub with the money and said he wouldn't have bet if he'd known. Apparently he's saving up for his own Nintendo Switch because *Animal Crossing* only allows one island per console and his little sister used all the island's resources for her character on the shared family Switch. Also, she called the island Arendelle. I have no idea what any of this means and I don't care.

My bet of two weeks overestimated Jodie and Melissa's commitment and didn't take into account the fact that Melissa's 25th birthday was only three days away. Her parents must have done alright for themselves because they bought Melissa a brand-new white Subaru Crosstrek for her birthday - which they could have presented to her at her apartment before or after work, but instead had it delivered to the front of our office with a giant red bow tied around it.

It was like one of those television commercials where the husband surprises his wife with a brand new Lexus in the driveway for Christmas. The ones that come on while you're watching television with your wife and you know she's thinking, 'I wish I was married to that guy' but you're fine because this year you splurged and got her a Huffy mountain bike and Rachael Ray nonstick saucepan & skillet set with bonus spatula and egg rings.

Coincidentally, Jodie also owns a Subaru Crosstrek. Hers is orange and a few years older though, with a shopping trolley ding in the passenger side door and a stained headliner from when she didn't see a speed bump while drinking a Starbuck's Frappuccino. Jodie financed her orange Crosstrek and still has two years of payments to make. Also, Melissa's Crosstrek has heated leather seats.

When people smile with genuine happiness, the voluntary contraction of the muscles that pull up the lips creates an involuntary contraction of the muscles that pull the cheekbones up, and the skin around the eyes in. It's a whole face party and the eyes are invited. Sometimes there's even a twinkle. Jodie's smile wasn't one of those smiles.

"Your parents gave you a Crosstrek for your birthday?"
"Yes."
"Oh wow."
"I know, right? I'm so happy right now."
"Me too. For you."

"First they pay off my mortgage and now this. Look, it even has personalised number plates that say MEL94."

"Yes, I see them. I considered getting personalized plates for my Crosstrek but then I decided they're a bit tacky."

"Tacky?"

"Oh, I didn't mean yours are. Just in general. I can't believe we both have the same car."

"Not really, mine's a newer model and has heated leather seats."

Generally when Melissa and Jodie have an altercation, it's difficult to ascertain who actually started the fight as there's an incremental progression from the first passing comment to raining fire. The increment count varies from fight to fight of course, based, I suppose, on how much shit Melissa or Jodie is prepared to put up with that day, but in this instance there weren't any increments between the heated leather seat statement and "Happy birthday slut, here's your cake."

Gary was in the foyer with Jodie and Melissa during the exchange. He didn't try to intervene though, the last time he attempted to separate the two - during a potted yucca fight over leather boots - he was elbowed in the throat and had to lie down in his office. This time, he just ran up the stairs and yelled, "Fight!" He didn't escape completely unscathed; a splatter of birthday cake struck his pants when he ran through the crossfire. He was pretty cross about it because he had a meeting to go to.

"It's completely unacceptable. I have an important meeting with Smucker's in fifteen minutes and my crotch is covered in cake icing. I tried wetting it and rubbing it off in the bathroom but if anything that made it worse. It looks like I dropped an icecream in my lap."

"No it doesn't, Gary."

"Yes it does."

"Honestly, it doesn't."

"Are you sure?"

"Yes, it looks more like a massive cum stain."

Gary has been at the agency for eighteen months but he still appears shocked and bewildered on a daily basis. His last job was working as an account rep for a fertilizer distribution company, which means he hasn't had a great deal of experience dealing with 'creative types'. I'm fairly certain he views us all as children - not just because he's the oldest employee at the agency, but because I've heard him referring to us on the phone as "brats who need a good spanking."

"Yes, I'll have Ben send you the copy this afternoon... no, you're thinking of David, Ben is the other man-child. They both have toy robots on their desks though... yes, they play with them."

Ben and I do have toy robots on our desks. We don't 'play' with them though. The collection started after Ben brought in a small tin robot for his desk, and I purchased a bigger robot - the robot from *Lost in Space* - for mine. A few days later, the robot from *Forbidden Planet* appeared on Ben's desk. It was three inches bigger than my robot, so I ordered a fifteen-inch ED-209 from the movie *Robocop*, and Ben ordered a twenty-inch robot from *The Iron Giant*. It was on. Within weeks, our desks were covered with cylons, daleks, cybermen, transformers, terminators, droids, gundams, and talking cars.

"Technically KITT isn't a robot, but okay."

"Why? Because he has wheels, Ben? He's more of a robot than Inspector Gadget."

"Please. KITT is just a car with artificial intelligence."

"Inspector Gadget is just a guy with gadgets."

"Lots of gadgets."

"By that argument, anyone holding a Swiss Army Knife is a robot."

"No, it would have to be a built-in Swiss Army Knife, Inspector Gadget's gadgets are built in."

"Just admit that Inspector Gadget is lame."

"He could beat KITT in a fight."

"Anyone with a wheel-clamp could beat KITT in a fight as long as they stayed clear of his doors, that's hardly the point."

"What is the point?"

"The point is, KITT is an artificially intelligent computer module in the body of a highly advanced robotic automobile, and therefore meets the definition of a robot."

"Fine, I'll accept that KITT is a robot if you accept that Inspector Gadget also meets the definition."

"Technically he's more of a cyborg. Would you agree, Gary?"

Gary doesn't have much of an opinion about robot cars and detectives with built-in umbrellas, which is surprising as he has an opinion about everything else. According to Gary, everything invented after 1970 is junk, anyone born after 1960 wouldn't last ten minutes in a war, and all music, barring that of legendary composer and pianist Billy Joel, sounds like metal objects being tossed into a dumpster. Apart from easy-listening tracks for the elderly, I have no idea what Gary does like. Maybe brown slacks and orderly queues?

To: Gary Wright
From: David Thorne
Date: Tuesday 8 September 2020 1.37pm
Subject: Quick question

Gary,

What do you like?

David

....

To: David Thorne
From: Gary Wright
Date: Tuesday 8 September 2020 1.49pm
Subject: Re: Quick question

I don't understand the question. What do I like about what? There was nothing attached.

To: Gary Wright
From: David Thorne
Date: Tuesday 8 September 2020 1.53pm
Subject: Re: Re: Quick question

Not what you like about something, something you like in general. What's something that tickles Gary's fancy?

....

To: David Thorne
From: Gary Wright
Date: Tuesday 8 September 2020 2.03pm
Subject: Re: Re: Re: Quick question

It's none of your business what I like. Is that a sexual question? Why are you asking? How would you like it if I asked you personal questions?

....

To: Gary Wright
From: David Thorne
Date: Tuesday 8 September 2020 2.11pm
Subject: Re: Re: Re: Re: Quick question

I'd be pleased that you were taking an interest. And no, it's not a sexual question. Unless you want it to be. I'll put the question another way: If you were filling out an online dating profile, what would you write in the field that states 'List your hobbies, likes, or interests'?

....

To: David Thorne
From: Gary Wright
Date: Tuesday 8 September 2020 2.26pm
Subject: Re: Re: Re: Re: Re: Quick question

If you're creating an online dating profile using my name you're going to be VERY sorry. This might be the kind of juvenile behavior you and Ben find amusing but nobody else does. Frankly, you both need to grow the fuck up and start acting your age.

I'm forwarding this correspondence to Mike.

....

To: Gary Wright
From: David Thorne
Date: Tuesday 8 September 2020 3.29pm
Subject: Re: Re: Re: Re: Re: Re: Quick question

Gary,

I'll just put down that you like brown slacks and orderly queues.

David

To: David Thorne
From: Gary Wright
Date: Tuesday 8 September 2020 2.34pm
Subject: Re: Re: Re: Re: Re: Re: Re: Quick question

No you won't. If you do, there will be serious repercussions.

....

To: Gary Wright
From: Irene Furtshower
Date: Tuesday 8 September 2020 2.53pm
Subject: Bslackgirl1943 has send you a message

Hi there Cutie,

Saw your online profile. I too am into brown slacks and orderly queues. Wanna hook up?

Irene X

P.S. I've attached a photo.

I flew with Gary to Tampa earlier this year, before the pandemic shut everything down, and it was the third worst business trip I've ever been on. Firstly, if you have a chance to visit Tampa, choose not to. The city is a shithole and everyone there is insane. Secondly, if you have to go to Tampa, don't go with Gary. It's like travelling with an angry geriatric five-year-old. He grumbles about everything, from the colour of orange juice to cloud density, and has never heard the term 'pick your battles'.

The flight from D.C. to Tampa is an easy two and a half hours, but in that short period Gary managed to reprimand a female passenger for wearing too much perfume, demanded the cabin temperature be raised because it was 'as cold as a well digger's ass in here', told a male flight attendant not to fuck with him because he knows karate, threatened to sue the airline for bumping his knee with a drink cart, and shouted at a child for crying. I'm not a fan of crying children on airplanes, but I've never had the inclination to yell, "For the love of god, someone smother it!"

I told the flight attendant that Gary had dementia and bought the mother a drink as way of apology. I also used the in-flight wi-fi to change my return seat so I wouldn't be sitting next to Gary.

During the Uber ride to the meeting, Gary loudly stated, "I was expecting a much nicer car. You'd think they'd have to meet some kind of standard."

During the meeting, Gary informed the client that her boardroom chairs were ugly, asked if their windows had ever been cleaned, and took his shoes and socks off.

"Sorry about this, he doesn't get out much."
"Yes I do. I'm very active."
"Belligerence isn't a sport, Gary. Put your shoes back on."
"I can't, my feet are swollen. Look."

The swelling was pretty bad; his feet looked like footballs with toes and appeared to be getting bigger by the minute. Apparently it's called edema. The client gave Gary a Benadryl and a cardboard poster tube to use as a walking cane, but Gary declared himself unable to fly or drive a vehicle, so I had to rent a car and drive nine hundred miles back to D.C. with him lying on the back seat grumbling the whole way. It was like a twelve-hour version of *Driving Miss Daisy* but in a Toyota Camry with Sirius XM and without the character development and eventual friendship. Just the bits where Miss Daisy complains about the bumps, the climate control settings, and her seat's lack of decent lumbar support. I haven't seen the movie, because I don't watch movies about old ladies being driven around in cars, but I assume Miss Daisy and Denzel Washington become friends, despite their differences, and team up to win a race or something. Also, Gary's bladder must be the size of a walnut because we had to stop every half-hour so he could use a restroom. I had to help him in and support him while he urinated, and he pissed on my leg twice.

"Are you sure there are no stations that play Billy Joel?"

"Yes, I checked. Just EDM I'm afraid."

"It's not even real music, it's just microwave button beeps."

"Yes, well, kids these days, huh?"

"I need to use a restroom."

"Again? We stopped ten minutes ago."

"I couldn't go while you were watching me."

"I wasn't watching you, Gary, I was checking your aim. Just use the empty Gatorade bottle I gave you."

"I'm not peeing in a bottle. I'm not an animal."

"Animals don't pee in bottles, Gary. They do, however, sometimes pee on people's legs."

"How many times do you expect me to apologise for the same thing? I said I'd pay for dry cleaning."

"That's not the point. My sock is squelchy and we still have six hundred miles to go."

"You should have packed a spare pair of socks to change into. It's the number one tip for flyers."

"Why would I pack socks for a meeting? It was meant to be a short flight there, short flight back. My itinerary didn't include driving across the country in piss socks."

"My itinerary didn't include being crippled. Sorry to be such a bother. Why don't you just pull over and leave me in a ditch. If I'm lucky, an alligator will eat me."

"It's tempting. Might be a little difficult to explain to Jennifer though. She'd probably make me fill out a form."

"Jennifer is nice."

"Yes, she's very pleasant."

"She's the only one I like at the office."

Jennifer was the first person I met when I started at the agency. We sat at the boardroom table, waiting for Mike to join us, and she asked me about kangaroos and big spiders and showed me photos of her daughter Cara on her first day at kindergarten and her husband Dan wearing a straw hat. Her eyes twinkled when she smiled and she laughed at my joke about screaming being Australia's official language. When Mike eventually arrived, thirty minutes late, Jennifer admonished him for his tardiness, but in a way that made it obvious they liked each other and had worked together for many years. She had to leave a short time later, to go to another meeting, but on her way out she placed a hand on Mike's shoulder and said, "I like him, offer him the position."

That was ten years ago. I've received my own fair share of admonishments from Jennifer in the last decade, but they've all been warranted and accompanied by an eye twinkle. I've never felt 'unliked' by her. It's a rare trait as everyone I have ever known has disliked me at some point. Usually within the first few minutes. You are more inclined to avoid disappointing someone that likes you though, so maybe it's just some kind of HR mind trick.

"I like you."
"Right, well now that I think about it, these probably aren't the droids we're looking for. Easy mistake to make, they all look very similar. Sorry if I came across as antagonistic. I plan to work on my interpersonal skills and will strive to be the best me I can be."

Back when Simon still worked for the agency - before his girlfriend cheated on him and we became friends and he gassed himself in his car - upsetting Jennifer was the line neither he nor I would cross. She was a yard stick of sorts and as long as she was bemused by our antics, we were free to 'have at it'. Whenever either of us were on the verge of taking a prank too far, or had actually upset the other, Jennifer moderated as if she was King Solomon ordering babies be cut in half.

"I want him punished."

"I completely understand, Simon. Pretending to be you when emailing clients simply isn't acceptable."

"No, it isn't. Jason from Safelite Autoglass thinks I want to date his wife."

"Well, that's certainly grounds for dismissal. I'll speak to Mike about terminating David's position at the company immediately. We can't tolerate that kind of behavior. Thank you for bringing it to my attention."

"Oh, right, I wasn't saying he should be fired."

"That's very big of you, Simon. What do you believe would be a suitable punishment then?"

"I don't know, maybe a formal complaint?"

"Sure. Fill one out and I'll file it with the others."

"It just looks bad for the company."

"Yes, it does."

"He also told Kate from Purina that I can hold my breath for seventeen minutes because I'm part fish."

"Unacceptable."

I almost killed Simon once, which would have saved him the bother of doing it himself later. He'd had a late night and had fallen asleep at his desk, snoring softly with his head back and mouth open, so I stuck a pickle in his mouth. It was a spur of the moment thing and I thought it would funny to see him either bite into the pickle or spit it out in surprise. I wasn't expecting him to gasp and swallow it. It sounded exactly like a hamster being sucked up and blocking a vacuum cleaner hose. Simon's eyes opened, wider than I'd seen them before, and he stared at me in panic while grabbing his throat and doing a weird thing with his head like a chicken pecking at corn. I panicked as well and did an on-the-spot dance while shaking my hands in front of me. I'd like to think my panic was due to fearing for Simon's wellbeing, but it was probably the thought of having to explain his death afterwards.

"Yes officer, I've told him several times not to swallow pickles whole but he never listened. I would have attempted to give him the Heimlich maneuver but he had a thing about hugs, I think he was like seventy percent autistic."

It was Rebecca who saved the day. She was in the supply room next door, using the spiral binder, and heard Simon slapping his desk. Though short and petite, weighing maybe a big bag of concrete and three cats if that, Rebecca lifted Simon out of his chair, swung him around, and administered the Heimlich maneuver with one big squeeze. The pickle popped out like a cork and hit the far wall of his office.

It would have been a lot easier for me if Simon had died that day. Jennifer told me I'd crossed a line and that she wasn't cross, just disappointed. Nobody wants to hear that. I also had to attend an occupational health and safety course and sign an F26-B formal complaint form stating I had read and understood section 5C of the employee agreement about skylarking. For Secret Santa that year, I gave Simon a jar of pickles but nobody thought it was funny.

Hats off to Rebecca though, she stepped up when I froze. That's difficult for me to admit because I don't like her. She has a huge forehead like Robocop or Ellen Page, and she always has to 'one up' people.

"Sorry I'm late, Rebecca. I didn't get to bed until 2am."
"I didn't get to bed until 8.59am and I still managed to make it to the 9am meeting on time."
"That doesn't seem possible but okay. You do live closer though. I had to drive here in heavy traffic."
"I had to walk."
"Your car is in the parking lot. I parked next to it."
"That's not mine. I walked here this morning. In shoes made out of crushed glass and thumbtacks."
"That's highly unlikely, why would anyone do that?"
"And it was snowing."
"It's the middle of summer."
"And a bear attacked me. It tore off both my arms."
"I can see you have arms, Rebecca."
"I guess I just have more respect for other people's time."

Rebecca has only lived in the United States a few years longer than I have. She was born in Germany which may explain her unblemished attendance record, crisp outfits, and no-nonsense approach to hairstyles. I'm not a fan of hair buns in general, they look like you're balancing a coconut on your head, but surely someone at some point has suggested bangs to Rebecca. I don't wish to harp on about the size of her forehead, but, honestly, you could land a helicopter on it. It's also a well-established fact that Germans have no sense of humour.

"Hans, I have a very funny joke for you."
"Proceed, Fritz."
"There is something on your foot."
"There is? I see nothing."
"It is your shoe."
"That is a very clever joke. You could be a professional comedian. Do you have another?"
"Yes. How many Dutch people does it take to screw in a lightbulb?"
"It is not a complicated task so my guess is one."
"Incorrect. The answer is none. Dutch people do not own houses with electricity."
"Because they are poor?"
"Yes."
"That is a very funny joke. I dislike Dutch people."
"Yes, they drive their camping buses incredibly slow along our Autobahn during the summer holidays, thus causing us to brake our BMW's hard."

Holly's mother, Maria, is German. Very German. She's more 'Black Forest' German than 'designer furniture' German though. I'm not sure how Holly's father Tom met Maria, but he was stationed in Germany during his time in the army and probably saw her milking a goat or something.

"Sir, I love your daughter and wish to marry her. She will have a good life and new teeth. Here's a Hershey's Bar."

Maria is too young to have been a member of The Hitler Youth but, based on her unquestioning devotion to the current sociopath in the Oval Office, she'd have fit right in. She would have been the one with the most merit badges, the first to point out dissidents to officials, and, if Facebook had been a thing in that era, posted 'Share if you're proud of the Führer' memes several times a day.

"New merit badge, Maria?"
"Yes. It's my 'find a hiding Jew' badge. I'm working on my 'find a whole family of hiding Jews' badge."
"Well, I must be off. Buns to practice. Auf Wiedersehen."
"You forgot to say, 'Heil Hitler' and do the hand thing."
"Did I? "
"Yes. I now question your love of the Führer and intend to report you as a Jew sympathiser to the authorities. Your entire family will no doubt be interrogated and likely executed."
"Please don't. I love the Führer with all my heart."
"It was a joke."

During Simon's funeral service, Jennifer sat beside me and held my hand. It wasn't weird or uncomfortable, it was just her way of saying 'we' knew Simon and 'we' were there. I didn't even realise she was holding my hand until she let go when it was my turn to say a few words.

"I've never been to a funeral," Walter had stated. He hadn't known Simon but wanted to go. "What do I wear?"
"A wetsuit is fairly standard," I answered, "you've never been to a funeral?"
"No. Do I have to buy a suit?"
"You already have a suit. Wear the black one you wore to Mike's dinner party last week."

Before the pandemic, Mike and Patrick held dinner parties at their apartment fairly regularly. Patrick is a vegetarian, so none of the food is edible, but it was important to attend because if you didn't, everybody talked about you; "So, where's x tonight?" is code to begin a group evaluation of the absent person's personality, work ethic, hygiene, wardrobe, hairstyle, and likelihood of being the one who left a floater in the bathroom. There was an air about the office for at least a week when you missed a dinner, a circle you stepped out of. Those that attended had longer kitchen conversations, smiled knowingly when they passed each other in the hallway, made each other friendship bracelets. Comments such as, "Oh that's right, you weren't there, you missed out on a really great cucumber and pine-nut risotto," really meant, "We're all best friends forever and you might be getting fired."

"That's not a suit," Walter replied, "The jacket and pants don't match. The jacket has a herringbone texture and the pants are dark blue. That's why I sat down the whole night."

"I didn't notice and I doubt anyone at the service would care if you wore happy pants. I've seen people wear *beige* pants with a dark jacket and tie."

"I have to buy a tie?"

Walter was wearing cargo shorts and a Boba Fett t-shirt the day he arrived for his interview. He'd ridden his bicycle and was shown into the boardroom still wearing his helmet. I'd held back a chuckle and kicked Kevin under the table. We were holding the first round of interviews for Simon's replacement in Mike and Jennifer's absence. It would be a quick interview, I thought, wondering how Walter had even made the list. He was barely out of his teens and the position required an experienced designer - someone with 'an eye'. We chatted for a bit, then I asked to see his portfolio to get it over with.

"You better not have," Mike had said over the phone, "you're going to have to apologise and explain that you didn't have the authority to offer him the position."

"No, he starts Monday. I offered him the job because I didn't want him going to an interview anywhere else. You'll agree with the decision when you see his portfolio."

"It's that good?"

"I took it upstairs to show Jodie and she cried."

"Actual tears?"

171

"A pretty solid glisten."

"Jennifer's going to have a fit when she gets back, I get to pretend to be angry with you so she doesn't get angry with me. I'll write a stern email or something."

"That's fine."

"Have you seen Simon?"

"Yes, but I haven't told him we're interviewing for his replacement."

"Fuck him. You don't quit in the middle of a client meeting and expect your job to be waiting for you."

While in the middle of a client meeting - explaining to a rep from Kraft Foods why fourteen pages of text can't fit on the back of 320mL jar label - Simon stood, stated, "I can't do this anymore," and left. His dramatic exit was diminished somewhat when, despite having opened and closed the boardroom door hundreds of times before, he pulled and shook the handle for several seconds and yelled, "what the fuck is wrong with this door?" before remembering it swung outwards. Earlier that week, Simon had confided to Melissa that he was having 'relationship issues' so everyone knew within an hour that his gothic girlfriend Cathy had slept with a white-water rafting instructor.

Simon's father came in to collect his personal belongings a few days later and, when I asked how Simon was doing, he replied, "He'll be fine, what doesn't kill you makes you stronger."

Which isn't always true as I know someone who contracted Ross River Virus several years ago and he now needs to be pushed around in a wheelchair; moaning the whole time about his joints and inadequate ramp access. I visited him in his ground-floor apartment once but it was a miserable and forced conversation so I told him I had a present for him in my car, went to get it, and drove home.

"I don't think he expects his job to be waiting for him. He said he'd rather be stabbed than ever have to design a business card or logo again."

What's he going to do then?"

"Make bowls apparently."

"Make what?"

"Wooden bowls. He owns a lathe."

"No, I mean what's he going to do for money?"

"Sell bowls."

"To who?"

"People who like wooden bowls I assume. To put their keys and sunglasses in."

"He's going to starve."

Surprisingly, Simon hadn't starved. After creating a clean website and branding his product well, one of his bowls was featured on a website called Houzz and, shortly after, on a popular HGTV kitchen makeover program. He received over 1200 pre-orders for his 20-inch $430 shallow Maple-burl bowl named *Horizon* on the first day alone. I have one on my dining table to put keys and sunglasses in.

173

Simon and I hadn't gotten along very well when we worked together. We butted heads often, both of us looking for reasons to do so. He'd filed at least sixteen formal complaints against me and we'd sat through several meetings with Jennifer to resolve conflicts. He once threw a screwdriver, across two rooms with a corridor between, which embedded itself into a wall a few inches above my head. I could have lost an eye which would have prevented me from ever becoming a professional tennis player. It's easy to take depth perception for granted.

He'd thrown the screwdriver after discovering I'd removed all the screws from his office chair but, really, who gets back from lunch to discover a screwdriver and 46 screws on their desk and *still* sits down? It was meant to collapse into 16 pieces when wiggled but instead, he'd looked up at the air vent suspiciously and plonked himself down. What air vent takes 46 screws? I'd removed the screws in retaliation for him removing the exterior knob and spindle on the men's bathroom while I was in there earlier. I'd heard a rattle and yelled, "Occupied!" but hadn't guessed what was happening until I tried to leave. I had to kick the inside knob off and poke a plastic toilet brush handle into the square hole where the spindle had been to get out.

Removing the bathroom knob was retaliation for hiding half a tin of tuna in the air vent in Simon's office, which was retaliation for him changing the alert tone on my computer to a K.D. Lang song, which was retaliation for changing his

174

email signature to 'Bobby Beige, Fashion Expert', which was retaliation for him saying, "K.D. Lang rang, she wants her haircut back." I'd been feeling self-conscious about my new haircut before he even made the comment.

It was as much a surprise to Simon and I as everyone else that we became friends after he left the agency. Or maybe we'd been friends the whole time. Intertwined with the childish antics and bickering, had been a mutual love of design and a respect for the other's experience in the design industry. There was an undeclared ceasefire the moment discussion turned to a logotype's kerning, the appropriate grid for a layout, tweaks to turn a good design into award winning work. There were no niceties, no 'It's pretty good but have you thought of's', only junior designers require delicacy and praise. We ripped into flawed design like lions on a crippled antelope. It took me a couple of weeks after Simon left to stop walking into his office with proofs. The third time it happened, I emailed him to see how he was doing.

"You don't own a tie?"
"Well, one," Walter answered, "but it has a penguin on it."
"A small embroidered penguin?"
"No, it's a pretty big penguin. He's ice skating."
"Is it a Christmas tie?"
"No. Just a penguin ice skating tie."
"That should be fine then. If anyone asks if it plays *Jingle Bell Rock* when you squeeze it, you can say, 'No, it's not a

Christmas tie, it's just penguin ice skating tie.' Is the penguin wearing a scarf and beanie?"

"No... actually, it might be now that I think about it. It's been a while since I wore it."

"Last Christmas?"

"No, to a movie premiere."

"You wore a tie to a movie premiere?"

"I thought premiere meant you had to dress up. You know, with a red carpet and stuff. I'd never been to a premiere before."

"Was the movie *Happy Feet*?"

"No, I can't remember what it was called but it was about an Indian kid and a tiger in a boat."

"*Life of Pi*."

"No, it wasn't about pies. Just tigers and boats."

"And an Indian kid. The movie is called *Life of Pi*."

"No, I'm pretty sure it isn't. You must be thinking of a different movie. Can I borrow a tie?"

Walter was rather upset that I'd forgotten to bring him a tie so we stopped at Target on the way to the service. He made me go in with him, because it was my fault he had to, while Jennifer, Mike and Jodie waited in Jennifer's Prius. I didn't mind as it was cramped in the back seat, what with Jodie being pretty much circular. She's always on a diet but it's that one where it's okay to eat six hotdogs and a family-size bag of chips for lunch. Really, when all days are cheat days, they're just days. Nobody's swept up in the performance so just shut the fuck up and eat the cake.

Once, during a three-hour drive to an out-of-town client, Jodie ate four full size Snickers and a loaf of sliced bread.

Only the five of us from the office attended Simon's service. I thought there would be more but the others had 'stuff to do' or 'didn't really know him very well, you know, outside of the office'. There's a difference between having worked with someone and having worked together I guess, but I still found it disappointing. Perhaps if they'd gotten to known him better.

Simon's sister Janet had been the one who found him. She'd let herself in to his apartment and heard the car running in the garage.

I hadn't even known Simon was sad, let alone suicidal. I'd seen him the week before and he seemed fine. We drank beer and smoked cigarettes in his shed while shellacking wooden bowls. I can't remember everything we talked about that evening but I'm fairly certain the subject of running a pipe from his car's exhaust pipe hadn't come up.

"Why aren't we wearing gloves for this?" I'd asked.
"Because you wouldn't be able to feel the grain. You may as well be spraying it on if you're wearing gloves."
I held up stained hands, "What takes varnish off? My nails look like Melissa's teeth."
Simon passed me a metal can and a rag, "It's not varnish, it's shellac."

"That's not just the brand name?"

"No, varnish is a polymer, shellac is a natural product and food safe. It's actually an excretion from the female lac bug. It seals better than varnish or oil and gives a deeper, richer shine. I think it's worth the extra effort. I saw Cathy last week, did I tell you?"

"No."

"At the hardware store. She was in the checkout line."

"And?"

"And nothing. She didn't see me, I was behind a DeWalt power tool display. She was buying a shelving system."

"The wooden type or those wire ones?"

"The wire ones."

"Cheap arse bitch."

"Yeah, they're alright for linen cabinets though. They let the fabric breath. She looked good."

"Really? So she's given up on the whole gothic thing and lost 200 pounds?"

"Wiccan and no, but her hair's blue now. It's funny how girls move on a lot faster than guys."

"Yes, it is. I once asked Holly once how long it would be before she'd start dating again if I died and she said, 'not for at least three months'. Says a lot really. She'll probably be downloading Tinder at my funeral."

"I know, it's like they have a 'next' button... I wonder who helped Cathy put up the shelves."

I'm not sure I've ever been truly depressed. I've been sad of course, at times so sad it was almost unbearable, but I think depression might be something different. It might be a degree of sadness I haven't yet reached, or perhaps it isn't about sadness at all. Maybe it's an absence of any feeling. Like when a coworker tells you about their weekend or shows you photos on their phone of their cat.

Rebecca sews outfits for her cat Jack. I'm not sure why. I guess she was just sitting around one day and thought, "Fuck this shit, I'm forty and single, time Jack had a Peter Pan costume."

"And here's a close up showing the detail on his felt hat."
"Right, but what's it for?"
"What do you mean?"
"Is it for a costume party or something?"
"He's Peter Pan!"
"Yes, I can see that, but why?"
"Because it's adorable!"
"Okay."
"And here's one of him sleeping."

I've seen photos of Jack dressed as a pirate, a fireman, a cowboy, a fish, and a vampire without feeling anything. Not even pity for the cat. It's one of those fluffy ones with the pushed in face, the kind that stares at you with disgust as if to say, "Who invited you to Endor?" I'm not a fan of any cats but if I'm watching a news report about one being rescued from a burning building and it turns out to be the fluffy pushed in face kind, I'm particularly disappointed.

"What do you think?" asked Walter, holding the tie up for everyone to admire. It was dark blue with grey triangles.

"Very nice," Jennifer affirmed, reversing out of the parking space, "and very fashionable. It looks just like Mike's."

"No it doesn't," Mike frowned.

"It's the same colour."

"Your Prius is the same colour as my Lexus. That doesn't make it a Lexus. We should have taken my car. There's more leg room and it makes noise. I keep thinking you've stalled at traffic lights."

"I get almost fifty miles to the gallon."

"Who gives a fuck? Are you on food stamps?"

"It was a bit expensive," Walter continued, "but it was the best one there."

"How expensive?" asked Mike. We'd agreed to put it on the company credit card.

"Twenty-five dollars," answered Walter, "but it was definitely the best one."

"That's not expensive for a tie," said Mike, "the one I'm wearing cost over two hundred. It's the Ermenegildo Zegna Tokyo tie."

"I like mine better," replied Walter.

"That's because you're a fucking philistine," Mike replied.

"I like Walter's better too," I said.

"Bullshit you do, you wish you owned this tie. What are you wearing? A boring black tie. Is it even silk?"

"I think so, it's Ralph Lauren."

"Oh my god, nobody wears Ralph Lauren anymore. They sell it at TJ Maxx."

I actually like TJ Maxx. They have good soaps. There's a TJ Maxx in the same plaza as the supermarket where Holly and I shop. Sometimes she suggests popping in to have a quick look and I sigh and say, "Oh, okay then," but I'm actually quite pleased. While Holly browses, I head straight to the soaps and give each a good sniff. By the time Holly's done, with a trolley full of cushions, photo frames and designer dog toys, I'll have thirty soaps in a 'we're definitely getting these' pile and another ten or fifteen in a 'smell this, what do you think?' pile. There's a third pile but that's a 'I don't want this but check out the packaging' stack. We have an entire cupboard full of soaps at home. Sometimes I stand in front of it and open and close the door really fast so I'm fanned by the combined scents.

Actually, I've only done that once or twice, I usually have much better things to do. I didn't want to leave the impression that I just stand around at home wafting the smell of soap towards myself.

"There's nothing wrong with TJ Maxx," I said, "They have good soaps. I'm using a cantaloupe & oregano one at the moment."
"Do they have Penhaligon's?" Mike asked.
"Is that a Harry Potter thing? "
"Exactly."
"It's also a good place to buy socks, you can get a six-pack for five dollars. Or do you only wear two-hundred-dollar socks?"
"They're Mario Bresciani. Signature collection."

Walter was pleased with his tie and that's all that mattered. He tied and retied it several times on the way to Simon's service, perfecting the knot and length and looking down to admire it often. I glanced over at him and he gave the tie a little flap at me. I smiled and nodded, he smiled and nodded back proudly. I gave Walter a thumbs up, which was supposed to be the end of the exchange but he gave me a thumbs up in return then pointed at the back of Mike's chair and quietly mouthed the word, "Jealous."

Jodie, sitting between us and taking up far more than a third of the back seat, shook her head.
"What did you write in your speech?" she asked.
"It's not a speech," I replied, "Simon's dad just asked me if I'd say a few words."
"Okay, but what did you write?"
"I didn't write anything. I'm just going to wing it."
"Oh my god."

I'd only met Simon's father, Keith, once before - when he came to the office to collect Simon's stuff - but he approached our group and shook my hand like we were old friends. We gave our condolences and Jennifer gave him a hug, which was nice, then we all stood around in a circle nodding for a bit before Keith headed off to mingle. Simon's sister Janet waved from across a crowd of twenty or so people and made her way over. I'd met her a few times when she'd visited Simon's place to help pack bowls into boxes and print shipping labels, but we hadn't talked much. She worked as a caregiver, whatever that means, for a retirement home that had been on the news a few years earlier for reportedly mistreating old people. I can't recall exactly what the accusations were but it had something to do with residents being washed with towels soaked in petrol to get rid of bed sores or something. It turned out to be only one resident, and methylated spirits not petrol, but he did have to go to the hospital with minor burns. I remember watching a news report at the time; the reporter approached a group of Cribbage players at a table and a wrinkled old lady looked up, clasped her hands together, and asked, "Are you here to save us?"

I mean, come on, it's not Hollywood, Edith, no need to ham it up. Suck on another Werther's and move your plastic pegs, everyone's had enough of your nonsense.

"Interesting choice of photo."
"Sorry?"
I nodded towards an easel displaying a large image of Simon smiling. He must have been 15 or 16 when the photo was taken and was wearing a McDonald's uniform.
"Was it his first day at work?"
"I like that photo," said Janet defensively, "what's wrong with it?"
"I'm not saying there's anything wrong it, just that it's an interesting choice. It's like an employee of the month picture, or a 'before' photo from a Proactiv advertisement."
"Okay."

"You couldn't find a more recent one?"

"No, not one where he looked so happy."

"Oh, right. Can't argue with that. Probably best not have a photo of him looking sad because... you know..."

"Yes."

"The suicide."

"Yes, I knew what you were referring to."

"I feel bad for mentioning it now. The photo I mean... and the suicide."

"It's fine.

"So how have you been?"

"It's been a difficult week."

"Yes, I'm sure it has. I meant generally though."

I'm not great at small talk. The key is to ask questions and show genuine interest in the answers but who has genuine interest on tap? Even if I manage to keep it up for a couple of rounds, eventually the facade cracks and we stand around nodding until someone says, "Well, I might go grab one of those toothpicks with a piece of cheese and an olive stuck on it before they're all gone."

Mike nudged me, "Check out the tragedy near the iced tea table," he whispered, "it's like *The Addams Family* cosplay."

She was all in black with a brimless 50's hat and black lace veil. Her velvet dress stopped just above the knees showing fishnet stockings and 12-hole Dr. Martens boots. Her back was towards us but I knew who it was instantly.

The first time I met Cathy was at a paintball game. There was a bit of contact back and forth between her and I after that in regards to medical expenses, but she'd signed a waiver so didn't have a case. For those unfamiliar with Paintball games, it's exactly like those medieval gatherings where a group of people named Timothy and Geoffrey don chainmail and rush at each-other in the forest with wooden swords. Except with guns that shoot things that look like those little balls you put in the bath. The ones that dissolve and make the water smell nice that generally come with a bar of soap in a little wicker basket wrapped in cellophane that you give as Christmas presents to people you couldn't care less about. I received one a couple of years back as my office 'Secret Santa' present and it still had a little tag attached with gold ribbon that read, "To Sarah, Merry Xmas 04."

I attended a medieval gathering once but only because my friend Geoffrey needed a lift. People who participate in medieval gatherings don't tend to own vehicles. I sat in my car the entire time to avoid being asked, "Whateth is this strange garb thou weareth?"

Adding 'eth' to the end of a word doesn't make it medieval, it makes it stupid. After about an hour of watching Geoffrey leap out from behind trees and whack people with his sword, I wound down the window and yelled, "How long are you going to be Geoffrey?" and he yelled back, "That's *Sir* Geoffrey, my goodeth fellow."

I'm fairly certain nobody in mediaeval times said the word 'goodeth' and there is no way Geoffrey would have been a knight if he'd been born in mediaeval times. He'd be the one being whacked by knights for not growing enough potatoes and making up words. After a hard day's work and several whackings, he'd lay down in the soil, cover himself with straw, and go to sleep imagining all the things he would do to the knights if he were a wizard.

The second time I met Cathy was at one of Mike and Patrick's dinner parties. She was only there for about five minutes and Simon was banned from ever inviting her again. You don't visit someone's house for the first time and throw a bowl of spinach & artichoke dip across a room, even if someone does ask you if you're just stopping by on your way to an Insane Clown Posse concert. We were civil the third time we met, there were other people in the line at Subway, so I just gave her my order and closely watched her make my footlong sub in case she tried to give me old lettuce.

The fourth time we met was at Simon's house. Cathy turned up unexpectedly and wanted to talk to Simon privately. I left. They tried getting back together but it only lasted a week. Simon couldn't get past her infidelity and Cathy hadn't exactly kept herself chaste since. Simon checked her phone while she was in the shower one morning and found several messages containing photos of her vagina sent to a fellow sandwich artist. They were taken in the Subway bathroom so I hope the hand washing procedures are enforced.

"Jesus Christ, that's Cathy" I sighed, "What the fuck is she doing here?"

The attendees, mostly elderly, had left a clearing of several feet around her. Possibly to avoid being singed should she suddenly conjure Satan. If I hadn't known Cathy, I might have felt sorry for her. Probably not though. She turned, recognised our group, and headed towards us. I turned away quickly.

"Goddamit. Pretend we're in the middle of an important discussion."
"About what?"
"Yes, I agree, traditional Haida art certainly does display many of the components found in modern logo and corporate identity design..."

Cathy touched me on the shoulder, I turned giving what I hoped was a 'slightly annoyed at being interrupted' look.

"Oh, hello Cathy."
She pantomimed a sad face and held out her arms as if expecting me to rush into them.
"Sorry, I don't do hugs. I have a thing."
"About hugs?"
"No, just a thing. What can I do for you?"
"I just wanted to say hello."
"Hello." I turned back to Mike, "So, as I was saying, you have to connect the green wire to the copper ground, otherwise it

might give you a shock."

"There's no need to be rude," Cathy stated at a volume above the general level of the room, "I'm grieving too you know."

A few people looked our way.

"Yes," I replied, "you certainly look the part. Were they having a hat sale at Widows'r'us?"

"No, asshole," Cathy puffed out her veil, "I bought it on Amazon. What's your problem?"

"Apart from the level of your voice right now?"

Cathy looked around, noticed the stares. She lowered her voice and leaned in, "I knew Simon a lot longer than you did, I've got just as much right to be here as you."

"Nobody said otherwise, I'm just surprised you bothered."

"Why wouldn't I? I cared about Simon very deeply."

"Not as deeply as you took that white-water rafting instructor's cock."

"Is there a problem?" Simon's father asked, approaching with his brow furled.

Jennifer stepped in, placed a hand lightly on his back, "There's no problem at all, Keith. Emotions just running a little high, you understand. David and Simon became close friends over the last six months and he's just a little protective and emot..."

"We were a lot closer," Cathy interrupted.

Jennifer pursed her lips, "It's not a competition, Cathy, I'm sure you and Simon shared a very special connec..."

"We were fireflies."

"Sorry?"

"It's from my poem. For the service."

"Dear lord," I said.

Jennifer pinched my arm. I flinched.

"Mike," Jennifer said, "weren't you and David about to head outside for a quick cigarette before the service begins?"

"No," Mike replied. Jennifer glared.

"Fine," Mike sighed, pushing me towards the door, "We'll be right back. In the meantime," he pointed to Cathy, "don't let Jizzo the Clown anywhere near the dip bowls."

I'm not a huge fan of poetry. I'll accept the argument that it's an art form - being an expression of the imagination - but by that broad definition, so are Etch-A-Sketch drawings and Magic Aqua Sand sculptures. I don't think anyone *really* likes poetry, apart from the ones writing it, and they only *really* like their own. People might declare they *really* like poetry but if pressed to name their favourite poem it's generally a struggle.

"Oh, um, probably the one about a tree or *The Road Less Travelled*. It's a classic."

"The 1978 book of psychology and spirituality by M. Scott Peck?"

"No, the poem version. I had to read it in school. It's about a guy who's taking a walk and chooses an overgrown path. It's a metaphor for not worrying about ticks."

"Do you mean *The Road Not Taken*?"

"No, that's a movie about a dad and his son who have to escape from cannibals after the apocalypse. I think Liam Neeson was in it."

We were seated three rows from the front. Cathy sat in the front row defiantly, dabbing her eyes with a handkerchief because that's what they do in the movies. Simon's coffin, closed, was on a raised pedestal behind a podium. It was honey pine, which Simon wouldn't have been pleased about.

Walter leaned over, pointed and whispered, "Is he in there?"
"No," I replied, "That's a truck driver named Larry."
"Alright. Just asking. I didn't know if they put him in there afterwards. To make it lighter to carry around."
"It lowers after the service and is cremated. They don't pause the service to carry the body in and plonk it in."
"It's weird that he's in there though."
"Yes, it is."

The man in the blue suit took the podium and thanked us for coming before speaking of Simon's life - a life 'short but very bright.' He spoke of Simon's childhood, his collection of hand painted *Lord of the Rings* figurines, his talent for 'pottery' and the lives he'd touched. It was standard fare but professional. Empty but delivered with warmth.

"And now," the man in the blue suit said, "one of Simon's close friends is going to say a few words...."
As I began to rise out of my seat, Cathy leaped up and whispered something to the man.
"Oh, apparently this young lady..."
"Cathy."
"Cathy has written a poem she'd like to share first."

Stepping aside from the podium, Cathy took his place. She cleared her throat, dabbed her eyes dramatically, and unfolded a piece of paper.

"Fireflies," Cathy said, pausing for another eye dab.
"I was searching, calling.
You called back, mirroring my pitch and luminosity.
I bobbed and flickered towards you.
You bobbed and flickered towards me.
We met halfway on a branch and embraced.
Who knows how long fireflies live?
A night? An eternity? Does it matter?
For a night or an eternity, our lights were twice as bright."

Cathy folded the piece of paper and gave the pantomime sad face again. Waiting, I suppose, for applause. Perhaps a standing ovation. She added a little nod.

"Okay, thank you," said the man in the blue suit, taking the podium again and indicating for Cathy to take her seat. She dabbed and nodded. Halfway back to her seat, she turned and returned to the podium, bending the microphone towards her, "I printed out extra copies of the poem if any of you would like one to take home. Just come and see me afterwards. They're free."

The man in the blue suit waited until Cathy was sitting before continuing this time, "And now one of Simon's friends is going to say a few words. David?"

I waited for a moment to see if Cathy would leap up again, then made my way to the podium.

"Okay, firstly, my condolences to Simon's family. For his loss and that poem. I Googled 'how long do fireflies live' on my phone while Cathy bobbed and flickered back and forth from the podium and apparently it's two months if anyone was wondering."

Cathy glared at me. I heard Mike chuckle.

"Secondly, Simon enjoyed woodwork, bowl turning to be specific, not pottery. He and I spent many late nights in his shed fulfilling the hundreds of orders he received for his bowls. I wasn't allowed to use the lathe but I became quite good at shellacking. The trick is to rub it into the grain with your fingertips even though it would be a lot easier to spray it on. His attention to detail, even the smallest of details, was infuriating at times, but it was what made Simon *Simon*. It was why he was good at whatever task he undertook, be it a two-hundred-page annual report with Venn Diagrams or turning a simple wooden bowl. He cared. I once asked him why he bothered doing a fourth coat of shellack on the bottom of bowls when it would never be seen and he replied, 'If a job's worth doing, it's worth doing well.' Which was a bit annoying as I'd quoted that years earlier to him regarding items super-glued to his desk and he'd just stolen it. I shellacked the bottom of bowls a fourth time while we drank Amstel Light and argued about design and music and pizza toppings. He was happy when he was working in his shed. Happier than he had ever been working as a graphic designer at our agency. In a way, he had Cathy to thank for that, if she hadn't had sex with a white-water rafting instructor while on holiday with her sister, it's unlikely he would have quit."

Several people whispered to each other. Cathy sunk low in her seat, her double chin quadrupled and her face scowled.

"Thankfully, he got over the breakup fairly quickly. It was only a matter of days before he met Emily, a model, and they began dating. She was intelligent, beautiful, creative and likeable - attributes he had failed to find in his previous relationship."

"He's making this up," Cathy protested. The man in the blue suit indicated for her to be quiet. Cathy crossed her arms and made a face that I assume was meant to be menacing but looked more like she was either pushing out a really huge turd or sucking one back in.

"Yes, Emily certainly was great. We all liked her a lot. She also wrote poems. Good poems though, I believe she was published. Simon was torn when her modelling career demanded she move to Paris for a year. There was talk of him moving with her but he had his successful bowl turning career to think of. The night before Emily left, we held a going away party for her and Simon proposed. She said yes and I've never seen two people so happy. Long distance relationships aren't easy but they had found their soulmates, each other's firefly if you will."

Cathy mouthed the words, "Fuck you."

"Sadly, Emily never made it to Paris. During a six-hour stopover in Indonesia, she decided to take in the sights and while exiting Changhangtang airport, was run over by a rickshaw. It's easy to only look left when you've grown up driving on the right. I was with Simon the evening he received the news that she had passed away. Being here today, we are all aware of the result of his grief, his decision that he couldn't continue without her. I'll miss Simon but I'm glad he found happiness, regardless of the outcome. None of us know how long we have, a night or an eternity, and finding happiness, no matter how brief, is all we can really hope for. I'll finish up with that but please, if we could, a moment's silence for both Simon and Emily."

Everyone bowed their head except Mike and Jennifer, who were shaking theirs, and Cathy who stood and yelled, "None of that happened."
"Please, Miss," the man in the blue suit grabbed her arm, "I'm sorry, but I'm going to have to ask you leave."

Cathy wrestled from his grip and stomped up the aisle, giving Mike the finger as she passed. I heard him say, "Go make me a sandwich, bitch," as she pushed through the door, slamming it with all her strength behind her. It had some kind of shock absorber on it and only made a 'pff' sound. I made my way to my seat and the man in the blue suit took the podium once again.

"Ladies and gentlemen, I apologise for the interruption. David, thank you for sharing those insights into Simon's life with us. It truly is better to have loved and lost than never loved at all. We will now play a song by Simon's favourite band, followed by the committal of the body."

They played a Dave Matthews track. I have no idea which one as they all sound the same. It's guitar-based elevator music that people with beards and beanies listen to while drinking Pabst Blue Ribbon and vaping in their friend Steve's bedroom. They nod along as they flick through mountain biking magazines and discuss CamelBak® water bottles and spoke tightening tools. Thankfully the song was killed halfway through and with a few words, a clank and whirring noises, Simon's coffin lowered into the platform and was gone.

"Is that it?" asked Walter, "we don't get to see it burn?"
"What? No, it goes into a furnace."
"I thought it was going to be like a fire pit. That would have been a lot better."
"Yes, we could bring beer and sausages on a stick."
"I didn't know Simon had a hot girlfriend. That's sad about the rickshaw accident."

Jodie took a handful of cheese and olive toothpicks with her 'for the road' on the way out. Keith shook our hands and thanked us for coming. He told me he had been stationed in Indonesia during his days in the military and didn't recall an international airport named Changhangtang. He smiled when he said it though.

"Here's to Simon," Mike said, raising his mojito, "he was a fucking idiot at times but he was good at his job."

We raised our glasses and drank as Mike indicated another round to the bartender. Walter dabbed at his tie with a tissue dipped in water; he'd leant across the counter and dragged it through a bowl of salsa. He was pretty upset about it, there was talk about taking it back and pretending the stain was there when he bought it and swapping it for another.

Jennifer raised her glass of Sauvignon Blanc, "He was the only one who ever did his timesheets on time."
"Yes," agreed Jodie, "and vacuumed his office carpet before leaving each day."
We laughed and drank to that.
I raised my Amstel Light, "Here's to the sixteen written and thirty-eight verbal complaints he made against me."
"It was a lot more than that," replied Jennifer, "Probably closer to a hundred."
We drank to a hundred complaints.
Walter raised his vodka & orange, "Here's to Emily."
"Really, Walter?" Jennifer said. We drank anyway.

We stopped at Jennifer's house on the drive back, because Mike wanted to see her new floorboards. I'd overheard Jennifer say something about moving furniture for new flooring to be put in, but I hadn't paid much attention. Whenever I hear the words 'moving' and 'furniture', I immediately find something else to do. As far as I'm concerned, if you can't afford movers, you probably don't have nice furniture, so just throw it out and get nice furniture after you move. No, I don't want to help you load your tattered green velour couch onto a rented trailer. Burn it.

I was roped into helping my friend Joseph move last year. After we'd loaded an open trailer with rickety dining room furniture, boxes of musty clothes, and a stained mattress, I asked him if we were taking it to his new place or to the dump. Apparently his grandfather had hand-made the kitchen furniture but I'm not sure what that has to do with anything. Sorry your grandfather was a shitty carpenter and too poor to buy nice stuff. Should we kick the legs off before throwing it into the trailer with the rest of the junk or toss it in as is?

It was the first time I'd been to Jennifer's house; a large Victorian era home with tall windows and high ceilings that she and Dan had renovated together. It was bright and airy inside, with fresh lillies in a vase and family photographs on bookcases and walls. Most of the photos were of their daughter Cara, but there was another young boy in several of the frames.

"Who's this kid?" I asked.

"That's Blake," Jennifer smiled, "Our first born, Cara's older brother. He died six years ago. He would have been about Seb's age now."

'Fuck, I'm sorry, Jennifer, I didn't know."

"It's fine. He was diagnosed with osteosarcoma, a type of bone cancer, and spent four years in and out of hospitals before we lost him."

"Jesus."

"No, fuck Jesus."

Apparently Jennifer and Dan met through their church and were once quite religious. Neither believed in invisible sky wizards anymore. Some people look to religion when they're lives are torn apart, some people grow the fuck up.

I believed in a God up until I was about five. The westernised version, not the Chinese wind and soup Gods or the Roman sea and lightning ones. I remember kneeling by my bed, hands clasped, begging God to give me a Spirograph. They were advertised on television in the late seventies and I'd decided I was going to be a professional spirographologist. Children are easily indoctrinated; if you could avoid outside influences and you were a bit of dick, you could easily produce an adult that 'knows' we are made of malleable rocks and came from the planet Scotchtape in a rocket made out of whipped cream propelled by farts. Even *with* outside influences, it's easy to indoctrinate a child using a reward system or punishment. I believed in Santa Clause and the tooth fairy because there were presents and cash involved. I believed in a God because if I didn't, I was ten times more likely to be hit by a car while I was riding my bike or become a homosexual. My grandmother was the one who told me that. She was a narrow-minded woman who hated Arabs, atheists, Jews, homosexuals, men with beards, Asians, women who wore eyeshadow, and Indians. Indians from India, not Native American Indians - though she probably hated them as well. She once told me that 'people like us' have white skin because God created us from the purest clay, and that Indians have dark skin because they were created out of poo. That's why they smell bad and are poor. I'm not sure why being made out of poo made them poor, but questioning my grandmother about anything meant having to read passages from her bible as it 'contained all the answers'. Her leather-bound bible was about the size of a toaster oven, with several hundred sticky notes poking out the sides making the volume even thicker. Many of the sticky notes were colour-coded, with yellow referencing passages that justified intolerance, blue referencing those who should be stoned to death - such as homosexuals, adulterers, and atheists - and pink referencing passages that came in handy whenever she needed to make anyone feel bad about themselves. A lot of the sticky notes had names written on them and why the passage was appropriate, for example: *Cheryl Phillips - blue eyeshadow* marked a passage about sexual immorality, and *David Thorne - sultanas* was attached to a passage about thieves and swindlers; I'd once lied about eating a box of sultanas my grandmother was planning to use in a fruit cake.

It was the story about Noah's Ark that first sparked my doubt in theological accuracy. For some reason I had no problem with magic and invisible beings, but fitting that many animals on one boat just didn't sit right. I couldn't get a straight answer on the size of the boat, just that it was 'really big' and when I pressed my grandmother on the logistics of fitting two of every animal - and all the supplies they'd require - on even a 'really big' boat, she changed the whole story and informed me that God shrunk the animals to the size of mice as they entered the ark, then made them full-sized again when they departed. I hadn't been told this earlier, and there was nothing about shrinking the animals in the bible.

It was at that moment I realized my grandmother was just making shit up as she went along. And that a lot of the stuff she made up was to justify her opinions and prejudices. Indians weren't made out of poo, millions of animals can't fit on a boat, and the only person who gave a fuck if Cheryl Phillips wore blue eyeshadow was my grandmother.

Cheryl Phillips was my grandmother's neighbour and she was nice. She had a Saint Bernard named Harry and one day when I jumped the fence to play with him, Cheryl gave me a glass of Coke and told me dogs have a sixth sense about people and can tell when they're kind and good; that's why Harry liked me. Which was nonsense of course, Harry liked everyone, but it was a nice thing to say. She asked me if I wanted to take Harry for a walk and we strolled around the block with Harry on a leash. It became a regular thing after that. This was a few years before my family got a dog and I grew quite attached to Harry. At some point, Cheryl hurt her foot and had to wear a big boot. She paid me to walk Harry after school while she recovered; I would have done it for free but she insisted. It was technically my first job and, with the money I earned, I bought a Spirograph. God wasn't going to bring me one, because he wasn't real, and when I'd asked my parents for one, my father said, "I'm not wasting money on wiggly circles. Just trace around a cup."

When Harry died - I think he had cancer - I helped Cheryl bury him in her backyard. We had to dig a pretty big hole, Saint Bernards aren't lap dogs, and it took us a few hours. After the dirt had been patted down, Cheryl held my hand and we just stood there looking at the mound.

"What happens to him now?" I asked.
"Worms eat him," Cheryl said, "then birds eat the worms and feed their babies with them and Harry becomes a part of all the other animals in the world. That's his job now."
"He doesn't go to Heaven?"
"Do you think he goes to Heaven?"
"No. There's no such thing."
"No, but it's nicer that way. It makes the time we shared more valuable."

Cheryl didn't believe in God, which meant, according to my grandmother, she had no moral compass.

It could be argued that those without a moral compass are the only ones who need written directions on how to act and treat others, but I won't go into that. I will say though, I have known a lot of people throughout my life and, regardless of the colour of their skin, sexual preferences, and amount of eyeshadow they wore, the majority have had a better moral compass than my grandmother ever did. I wasn't sad when I heard she died. The world is a better place without people like her. Years later, while helping my sister clean out her garage, I discovered my grandmother's bible in a cardboard box. It wasn't as large as I remembered but it took me two hands to lift and carry it to my car. When I got home, I removed the sticky notes, tore out several pages that had handwritten notes, put everything in a garbage bag, and threw it out with the rest of the trash.

There was an upright piano in Jennifer's hallway. It was old but in good condition. I asked if anyone played and Jennifer told me she used to. I prompted her to play something and, without sitting, Jennifer played the first thirty seconds or so of *Moonlight Sonata* flawlessly before shrugging and stating, "I'm a bit rusty."

"Well you'd never know," I replied, "That was beautiful. You could be a professional."

Jennifer laughed, "I'm not that good. I was the organist for our church though. It's the only part I miss. They had an old Hammond which was lovely to play."

"Why haven't you ever told me any of this?"

"You never asked."

To: All Staff
From: Jennifer Haines
Date: Friday 17 April 2020 11.42am
Subject: Production meeting

Good afternoon everyone,

I hope you're all well. Sorry I missed this morning's production meeting, I was up the entire night coughing.

No, it's not Covid. It's just a cold. Dan was feeling bad last week after he got back but he's fine now so I expect I'll feel better in a few days.

David, I still don't have your timesheets from the last two months. I understand you're busy with the Scott's rebranding and the annual report but Rebecca needs the timesheets to work out billables. The timesheets.doc file you sent was just a photo of a horse.

Gary, Mike approved your request for a new laptop. Everyone should be mindful that if they take their laptop anywhere not to leave it on the roof of their car.

Walter, thank you for changing your email signature. You spelled Graphic Designer wrong though. Designer has a G in it. The address and telephone number are also wrong.

Ben, can you please check Walter's signature is corrected? It reflects poorly on the agency if a client calls the number and gets his mom.

Also, I realize everyone is working from home at the moment and that you're unlikely to go into the office anytime soon, but I left a chocolate bunny on everyone's desk last week for Easter.

Please note: If you do go into the office, make sure the alarm is set and the door is locked when you leave. The alarm was off when I dropped off the bunnies. I made a sign and taped it by the alarm panel to remind everyone.

Have a good weekend. I'm going to Netflix and chill.

Jen

....

To: All Staff
From: Jennifer Haines
Date: Friday 17 April 2020 12.19pm
Subject: Netflix

Hi everyone,

Rebecca has just informed me that Netflix and chill doesn't mean what I thought it meant.

I meant all I intend to do today is put on Netflix, curl up with a blanket, and watch *Tiger King*. Not have sex.

Stay safe, Jen

"Just turn your camera on please, David."

"Fine."

"Thank you... are you in a hammock?"

"No, I'm using a background image like Ben does, but instead of a city skyline, I chose macramé."

"Yes, well this really isn't the time for jokes. Gary, can you hear me?"

"..."

"Okay, I'll call Gary after I've spoken to..."

"Yes, Mike..."

"Right. Well, most of you may have noticed Jennifer isn't on this call. I wanted to let you all know personally she passed away Wednesday night. I understand you may..."

"Over."

I held the hand of someone as they died once. Her name was Emma. It was late at night on a dirt road, about fifteen miles from a small town called Stockport in South Australia. I was only seventeen but had been drinking with three people I worked with on a horse-riding property. It was the kind of place where schools hold overnight 'Adventure Camp' excursions and I hadn't worked there long. I was in the back of a car with a guy named Michael, Emma was in the front with her boyfriend Brian, who was driving. Emma and Brian had been fighting because he'd been told off earlier that day by our boss for helping a young girl, twelve or so, onto a horse by clasping her bottom. There was a rule against touching bottoms and that rule had been added to the list of rules because Brian had a habit of doing it.

It was raining and the dirt road was slippery. Brian was speeding. Emma yelled for him to slow down. We all did. We were doing almost double the speed limit when Brian lost control. The wheels slid and I guess he overcompensated trying to correct the car's direction.

It happened quickly. We were travelling sideways when we hit the bank of a bend. If we hadn't slid, if it hadn't been muddy, I don't see how we could have taken the bend at that speed anyway. I told the jury that during Brian's court case.

The car flipped, rolled twice. Twice and a half really. It was like watching slow-motion footage. I heard screaming and breaking glass, watched bodies thrash back and forth, arms and legs fly up and down. The sound of the roof sliding fifty feet along the road, inches beneath my head, was deafening. Interminable. Then it stopped. It was dark and silent but for the clicking and flashing of emergency lights.

I was upside down with the seatbelt cutting into my waist. Managing to undo the buckle, I dropped onto my side. Michael did the same, landing on my head and causing my only injury. There was no glass in the windows so we crawled out. Brian was half way out of his window and Michael helped him to his feet while I knelt beside Emma's window.

Emma was still upside down but had slipped through her seatbelt. Her arm had flung out as the car flipped and was trapped under the roof. Sliding along the road had taken most of the flesh from it and ripped the bone from her shoulder - it was only held on by a few inches of meat and stretched skin. Blood poured from what looked like a fat hollow pasta noodle so I pinched the pasta noodle closed between my thumb and index finger and pressed my palm against the exposed meat surrounding it. Emma cried out, looking up at me frightened. She tried to pry my hand away with her free one. I grabbed it and held it away.

"You're bleeding," I told her, "I'm just trying to stop it."
"Am I going to die?"
"No, don't be ridiculous. Your arm is a bit fucked up though."
"Is it in my hair?" she asked.
"The blood? Yes."
"I straightened it this morning."

Her long blonde hair hung in a pool of blood on the ceiling of the car. There seemed to be an awful lot of it. Brian knelt beside us. "Are you okay, Emma?" he asked. His eyes widened and he put his hand over his mouth. Vomit sprayed out between his fingers, splashing the side of my face and neck as he stood and stepped back. Michael took his place, staring at Emma's arm. He put his hand on my back and said, "I'll go and get help."

This was before mobile phones were a thing. They existed, but came with a case that you carried over your shoulder with a strap and only American businessmen on television had them.

"Okay, be quick. And take him with you." I nodded towards Brian who was twenty feet away, punching a speed limit sign. I heard Michael yell something at Brian and watched them sprint off down the dark road. Brian stopped and ran back. "I don't have my license," he said, "Will you tell them that you were the one driving?"

"Go and get help, Brian."

"But will you?"

"No."

Brian called me a cunt, then turned and chased after Michael, disappearing into the darkness.

"Are you alright?" Emma asked.

"Me? I'm fine. Everyone's fine but you. Didn't anyone ever tell you to keep your arms inside the vehicle at all times?"

"Is that a joke?"

"It was meant to be. Sorry."

"That's okay. Am I going to lose my arm?"

"I don't know. Maybe they can stitch it back on. Does it hurt?"

"Not really. It just feels cold. Brian will leave me if I only have one arm."

"Brian doesn't deserve you with two arms. Besides, if you do lose your arm, you can get a robot one. That would be pretty cool. I'd swap an arm for a robot one."

Blood was leaking through my fingers, running down my arm and dripping from my elbow. I was still holding her other hand.

"Emma, I'm going to let go of your hand because I need to use mine, okay?"

"No." She tightened her grip.

"Alright, I'm going to press harder then. Does that hurt?"

"No but you're runnnn nyr hoodie."

"Sorry?"

"Ruining your hoodie. M sorry. M really tired."

"It's an old hoodie and I don't think you're meant to go to sleep. They'll be back soon. It will probably take them twenty minutes to get into town and another ten for the ambulance to arrive. Talk to me until they get here. What kind of music do you like? What's your favourite band?"

Back then, at that age, most conversations could be started by asking what kind of music the person listened to. The type of music you embraced defined who you were, how you dressed, who your friends were. It was simpler. In your forties, you can't just walk up to people at networking functions and chat about your favourite bands. You have to talk about bathroom fittings and look at photos on their phone of the fire pit they just completed.

I meant to ask Brian at Emma's funeral who her favourite band was, but he wasn't there. They played Lou Reed's *Perfect Day* during the service but I don't know who picked it.

When Emma's parents asked if Emma had said anything before she died, I told them she had apologised for getting blood on my hoodie. They nodded as if this was somehow an acceptable answer. I didn't tell them that Emma had urinated and defecated. That she hadn't just gone to sleep, she'd convulsed. That her large brown eyes were open and I tried to close them but my fingers were covered in mud and blood and I got it all over her face, that I didn't know what to do so I just sat in the mud holding her hand, long after she loosened her grip.

Nobody held Jennifer's hand as she took her last breath. Everyone who dies of the Corona virus dies alone - instantly apparently. It's the worst part really. For them and the people who love them. "You'll die alone," is something said to horrible people, to infer that nobody cares about them and never will.

Jennifer died alone, her body was cremated, and, a few days later, Dan received a receipt in the mail containing a barcode that allowed him to collect Jennifer's ashes. There was no service. In lieu of flowers, Dan asked that a donation be made to ActBlue. Anger pushes other emotions aside so it can sometimes be a good thing.

He and Cara spread the ashes at Scott's Run Falls, a nature preserve only twenty minutes or so from their home. I've seen Facebook photos of Dan, Cara and Jennifer hiking there. I've never been but I understand it's a nice area with a creek running through it and trails that lead to a waterfall. It's where Dan and Jennifer spread their son's ashes when he died.

I went in to the office a few months later. I needed to spiral bind a document and the cheapest Trubind® I could find on Amazon was $139.95 - there were cheaper brands available but it took me three years to work out the binder at work and I'm not starting from scratch now. Someone really needs to make one that you just stick the paper in and push a button.

"And this is the spiral binder, David. Put these gloves and goggles on and I'll show you how to operate it."
"You don't just stick the paper in and push a button?"
"Hahaha. No. Stand well back while I while I prime the horbinator and insert the noid into the ferve. If you hear a noise like a ball bearing dropped into an empty glass, run. Don't look back, just run."

Mike refuses to use the spiral binder at all. The one time he tried, he carried the spiral binder outside and threw it in the dumpster. Melissa had to climb in to retrieve it - it's one of her job roles. Throwing office equipment and furniture into the dumpster is Mike's way of dramatically expressing distain for them, but it's become so commonplace that Melissa keeps a stepladder and a robot arm with a claw - the kind that old people use to reach jars on high shelves - behind the dumpster.

"Fuck this laptop, it's going in the dumpster."
"Melissa is away today."
"First thing tomorrow then. Remind me."

It was weird walking around the office without anyone else there. Quiet and still. There have been other times when I was alone in the office, late at night and on weekends, but it didn't feel the same. It was if the office was paused, waiting.

Jennifer's alarm panel sign was just as bad as I assumed it would be. Her signs always were. I'm not sure how any sane person could consider the *Jurassic Park* typeface - with a rainbow border and clip art of a cartoon turtle eating an ice cream - appropriate for the entrance of a branding agency with minimalist decor. Usually when Jennifer put up signs - and there have been a few - I replaced them with clean Helvetica versions within the hour. I left her alarm panel sign as it is though. It's not as if any clients are going to see it anytime soon.

Mike had collected Jennifer's belongings for Dan a few weeks after she died. Her office was empty of anything that had made it hers. The whiteboard had been wiped clean and a corkboard, once littered with photos and sticky-notes, was bare apart from a group of multi-coloured thumbtacks at the edge. For as long as I can remember, Jennifer had a plastic chinese cat that waved its arm on her desk. It was white with a gold bell and Mike complained regularly that it was tacky and didn't fit with the overall aesthetic of the agency. Jennifer would tell him not to look at it if it upsets him, and Mike would reply that it was impossible not to look at it because its moving arm caught his peripheral vision. The waving cat was now on Mike's desk. He'd taken the battery out though.

Gary's office was practically empty. At some point he must have gone back in to the office and taken his bookcase, printer, a plastic plant, and his desk. I know the desks have to be dismantled to fit down the stairs, so hats off to Gary for the effort.

I swapped Melissa's office chair with Jodie's. It's a thing with them. The last time Jodie took Melissa's chair, Melissa pulled her off it by her hair and they'd wrestled on the carpet. I also changed the height and recline settings on Walter's chair and rearranged Ben's robots into sexual positions. Inspector Gadget's gadgets actually came in useful.

Rebecca's office was as clean and orderly as it's always been. It also smelled fresh, possibly due to a bag of Damprid she'd hung on the inside of her door. It was good planning on her behalf as the rest of the building smelled a bit musty. I took the bag of Damprid and hung it in my office.

My office was the same as I'd left it; an organized chaos of folders, printouts, proofs, poster tubes, and robots. The only addition was a chocolate bunny and a yellow sticky-note, stuck to my monitor, that read, "Please do your timesheets. Thank you, Jen."

The clock on my office wall showed it was 10.15am. I looked out the window, at the bus stop across the street. Mrs Bus Stop, wearing her red coat and a matching red mask, was sitting alone.

JM sent me email this morning, asking if I wanted to go to Deer Camp this weekend. I told him I was nearing the deadline on this book but maybe next year. It was half true, I am nearing the deadline. He posted a meme on Facebook yesterday, of a sheep wearing a mask. I spent a few minutes writing a reply, hovered over the post button, then closed the browser window. Life's short. Sometimes you don't learn enough about people, sometimes you learn too much.

Afterword

To: Ross Amorelli
From: David Thorne
Date: Monday 16 November 2020 1.22pm
Subject: Galley

Ross,

I sent you a galley proof of the book. It's essentially the same as the final version but with 'galley' written across the cover. It should be there within a couple of days.

I'll also send the free copies in a week or so once the author copies arrive.

David

....

To: David Thorne
From: Ross Amorelli
Date: Monday 16 November 2020 1.47pm
Subject: Re: Galley

Awesome.

To: David Thorne
From: Ross Amorelli
Date: Wednesday 18 November 2020 12.02pm
Subject: wow

You really are a dickhead. Don't even bother sending me the free copies.

....

To: Ross Amorelli
From: David Thorne
Date: Wednesday 18 November 2020 2.16pm
Subject: Re: wow

You didn't like the edits?

....

To: David Thorne
From: Ross Amorelli
Date: Wednesday 18 November 2020 2.29pm
Subject: Re: Re: wow

Why would I? I was excited to have my foreword in the book. I told a whole bunch of people. And you didn't tell me you were going to include the emails about doing the foreword. I would have been a lot wittier if I'd known.

I liked the bit about karaoke night though.

To: Ross Amorelli
From: David Thorne
Date: Wednesday 18 November 2020 2.34pm
Subject: Re: Re: Re: wow

You read the book then?

....

To: David Thorne
From: Ross Amorelli
Date: Wednesday 18 November 2020 2.45pm
Subject: Re: Re: Re: Re: wow

I skimmed through. The first half was OK but then you just started copying and pasting stuff from your old books. I know I've read about Simon's funeral before and it was in a different style to rest of the book. There were almost no emails and most of the stories were about people dying.

For someone who writes humour, it's a pretty morbid book.

....

To: Ross Amorelli
From: David Thorne
Date: Wednesday 18 November 2020 2.51pm
Subject: Re: Re: Re: Re: Re: wow

It's been a pretty morbid year.

To: David Thorne
From: Ross Amorelli
Date: Wednesday 18 November 2020 2.57pm
Subject: Re: Re: Re: Re: Re: Re: wow

Yeah. Hopefully next year will be better. Have you found a replacement for Jennifer yet?

....

To: Ross Amorelli
From: David Thorne
Date: Wednesday 18 November 2020 3.02pm
Subject: Re: Re: Re: Re: Re: Re: Re: wow

No, we did have a possible candidate but Mike decided she was too short. He vetoed another candidate because she breeds koi. Apparently he's not a fan of "fish people".

....

To: David Thorne
From: Ross Amorelli
Date: Wednesday 18 November 2020 3.09pm
Subject: Re: Re: Re: Re: Re: Re: Re: Re: wow

Lol. By the way, you know how you wrote about moths in bread? I made toast after reading that and held the slices of bread up to the kitchen light and guess what I found?

To: Ross Amorelli
From: David Thorne
Date: Wednesday 18 November 2020 3.13pm
Subject: Re: Re: Re: Re: Re: Re: Re: Re: Re: wow

A moth?

....

To: David Thorne
From: Ross Amorelli
Date: Wednesday 18 November 2020 3.17pm
Subject: Re: Re: Re: Re: Re: Re: Re: Re: Re: Re: wow

No, nothing. You're a dickhead.

About the Author

David Thorne is an artificially intelligent talking electronic computer module in the body of a highly advanced, very mobile, robotic automobile - essentially an advanced supercomputer on wheels. His microprocessor, which is the centre of a self-aware cybernetic logic module, has 1,000 megabits of memory and one nanosecond access time, allowing David to think, learn, communicate and interact with humans in real-time. He also has an in-dash entertainment system that can play music and video, and run various computer programs including arcade games.

David is armoured with Tri-Helical Plasteel 1000 Molecular Bonded Shell plating which protects him from almost all forms of conventional firearms and explosive devices. He can only be harmed by heavy artillery and rockets. This makes David's body durable enough to act as a shield for explosives, ram through rigid barriers of strong material without suffering damage himself, and sustain frequent long jumps on turbo boost. The shell also protects him from fire. The shell is a combination of three secret substances entrusted to three separate people, who each know only two pieces of the formula. The shell provides a frame tolerance of 223,000 lb (111.5 tons) and a front and rear axle suspension load of 57,000 lb (28.5 tons).

David's voice synthesizer allows his logic module to speak and communicate. With it, David can also simulate other sounds. David's primary spoken language is English; however, by accessing his language module, he can speak fluently in Spanish, French and more. The module can be adjusted, giving David different accents.

David has a front scan bar called the Anamorphic Equalizer. The device is a fibre-optic array of electronic eyes, allowing David to see in all visual wavelengths, as well as X-ray and infrared. An Etymotic Equalizer allows David to hear sound through an array of audio sensors threaded throughout his interior and exterior, and an Olfactory Sensor allows David to smell via an atmospheric sampling device mounted in his front bumper.

David is powered by a turbojet, with modified afterburners and a computer controlled 8-speed turbodrive transmission. This helps him do 0–60 mph in 2 seconds. His turbine engine is primarily fuelled by hydrogen gas but his fuel processor allows him to run on any combustible liquid, even regular gasoline. His electromagnetic hyper-vacuum disc brakes provide a braking distance of 14 feet.

A pair of rocket boosters mounted just behind the front tires, allow David to jump into the air and pass over obstacles in the road. David also has retractable spoilers for aerodynamic stability, a grappling hook, flamethrowers mounted under his bumpers, a tear gas launcher, a microwave jammer, movable air inlets for increased cooling, and a top speed of 300 miles per hour. Other useful features include a passive laser restraint system, voice stress analyzer, bomb scanner, traction spikes, seat ejection system, medical scanner, tinted windows, and an ATM.

You found Albert, the Unfindable Crab.
Time will now collapse.

Printed in Great Britain
by Amazon

84879282R00130